THE SPIRIT OF
THE CHINESE PEOPLE

中国人的精神

辜鸿铭

外语教学与研究出版社

(京)新登字 155 号

图书在版编目(CIP)数据

中国人的精神:英文/辜鸿铭著. - 北京:外语教学与研究出版社,
1998.4
ISBN 7 - 5600 - 1449 - 6

Ⅰ.中… Ⅱ.辜… Ⅲ.散文 - 中国 - 英语 - 语言读物 Ⅳ.
H319.4:Ⅰ

中国版本图书馆 CIP 数据核字(98)第 10964 号

中国人的精神
辜鸿铭

* * *

外语教学与研究出版社出版发行
(北京西三环北路 19 号 100089)
http://www.fltrp.com.cn
北京外国语大学印刷厂印刷
开本 850×1168 1/32 5.5 印张
1998 年 5 月第 1 版 2000 年 6 月第 4 次印刷
印数:30001—40000 册

* * *

ISBN 7 - 5600 - 1449 - 6
H·817
定价:6.90元
如有印刷、装订质量问题出版社负责调换

出版说明

　　我们现在将英语作为一种"世界英语"（WORLD ENGLISH）来看待；于是，英语不再只是单纯的一门异族语言，它同时融合着不同民族的表达方式并折射其多姿的文化。一个世纪以来，有过这样的一位位中国人，他们以各自令人惊叹的完美英语，对世界解说着中国，对祖国表达着赤忱。如今，我们相信，还有更多的中国人胸怀一样的向往，因为，跨越世纪的开放中国需要引进，也需要输出。

　　我们出版中国人的英语著述，正是为有志于此的英语学习者树一个榜样，为下个世纪的中国再添一份自信，还为世界英语的推广呐一声喊。

　　选择辜鸿铭（1857—1928）的作品重排出版，当然不是宣扬他那不免乖张偏颇的行为思想，而是感动于他对中国传统文化的奋力捍卫；惊叹于他那登峰造极、令人仰止的英语造诣。辜鸿铭通英法德俄等多种外语，但他的著述多用英文，而其中尤以《中国人的精神》为著。《中国人的精神》原载 1914 年的《中国评论》，1915 年更名《春秋大义》在京出版，并很快被译成德文，一时轰动西方。本书力阐中国传统文化对于西方文明的价值，在当时中国文化面临歧视、中华民族遭受欺凌的境况下，其影响尤为特殊。当然，对于我们现在的读者，这首先该是一本极为宝贵的英语读物。

回忆辜鸿铭先生

罗家伦

在清末民初一位以外国文字名满海内外，而又以怪诞见称的，那便是辜鸿铭先生了。辜先生号汤生，福建人，因为家属侨居海外，所以他很小就到英国去读书，在一个著名的中学毕业，受过很严格的英国文学训练。这种学校对于拉丁文、希腊文，以及英国古典文学，都很认真而彻底地教授。这乃是英国当时的传统。毕业以后，他考进伯明罕大学学工程（有人误以为他在大学学的是文学，那是错的）。

回国以后，他的工程知识竟然没有发挥的余地。当时张之洞做两湖总督，请他做英文文案。张之洞当年提倡工业建设，办理汉冶萍煤铁等项工程，以"中学为体，西学为用"相号召，为好谈时务之人。他幕府里也有外国顾问，大概不是高明的外国人士，辜先生不曾把他们放在眼里。有一天，一个外国顾问为起草文件，来向辜先生请问一个英文字用法。辜默然不语，走到书架上抱了一本又大又重的英文字典，碰然一声丢在那外国顾问的桌上说："你自己去查去！"这件小故事是蔡孑民先生告诉我的，这可以看出辜先生牢骚抑郁和看不起庸俗外国顾问的情形。

民国四年，我在上海愚园游玩，看见愚园走廊的壁上嵌了几块石头，刻着拉丁文的诗，说是辜鸿铭先生做的。我虽然看不懂，可是心里有种佩服的情绪，认为中国人会做拉丁文的诗，大概是一件了不得的事。后来我到北京大学读书，蔡先生站在学术的立场上网罗了许多很奇怪的人物。辜先生虽然是老复辟派的人物，因为他外国文学的特长，也被聘在北大讲授英国文学。因此我接连上

1

了 3 年辜先生主讲的英国诗这门课程。我记得第一天他老先生拖了一条大辫子，是用红丝线夹在头发里辫起来的，戴了一顶红帽结黑缎子平顶的瓜皮帽，大摇大摆地上汉花园北大文学院的红楼，颇是一景。到了教室之后，他首先对学生宣告："我有三章约法，你们受得了的就来上我的课，受不了的就早退出：第一章，我进来的时候你们要站起来，上完课要我先出去你们才能出去；第二章，我问你们话和你们问我话时都得站起来；第三章，我指定你们要背的书，你们都要背，背不出不能坐下。"我们全班的同学都认为第一第二都容易办到，第三却有点困难，可是大家都慑于辜先生的大名，也就不敢提出异议。

3 年之间，我们课堂里有趣的故事多极了。我曾开玩笑地告诉同学们说："有没有人想要立刻出名，若要出名，只要在辜先生上楼梯时，把他那条大辫子剪掉，那明天中外报纸一定都会竞相刊载。"当然，这个名并没有人敢出的。辜先生对我们讲英国诗的时候，有时候对我们说："我今天教你们外国大雅。"有时候说："我今天教你们外国小雅。"有时候说："我今天教你们洋离骚。"这"洋离骚"是什么呢？原来是密尔顿（John Milton）的一首长诗 Lycidas。为什么 Lycidas 会变"洋离骚"呢？这大概因为此诗是密尔顿吊他一位在爱尔兰海附近淹死亡友而写成的。

在辜先生的班上，我前后背熟过几十首英文长短的诗篇。在那时候叫我背书倒不是难事，最难的是翻译。他要我们翻什么呢？要我们翻千字文，把"天地玄黄，宇宙洪荒"翻成英文，这个真比孙悟空戴紧箍咒还要痛苦。我们翻过之后，他自己再翻。他翻的文字我早已记不清了，我现在想来，那一定也是很牵强的。还有一天把他自己一首英文诗要我们翻成中文，当然我们班上有几种译文，最后他把自己的译文写出来了，这个译文是："上马复上马，同我伙伴儿，男儿重意气，从此赴戎机，剑柄执在手，别泪不沾衣，寄语越溪女，喁喁复何为！"英文可能是很好，但译文并不很高明，因为辜先生的中国文学是他回国后再用功研究的，虽然也有相当的造诣，却不自然。这也同他在黑板上写中国字一样，他写中国字常常会

2

缺一笔多一笔,而他自己毫不觉得。

我们在教室里对辜先生是很尊重的,可是有一次,我把他气坏了。这是正当"五四"运动的时候,辜先生在一个日本人办的《华北正报》(North China Standard)里写了一篇文章,大骂学生运动,说我们这班学生是暴徒,是野蛮。我看报之后受不住了,把这张报纸带进教室,质问辜先生道:"辜先生,你从前著的《春秋大义》(The Spirit of the Chinese People)我们读了都很佩服,你既然讲春秋大义,你就应该知道春秋的主张是'内中国而外夷狄'的,你现在在夷狄的报纸上发表文章骂我们中国学生,是何道理?"这一下把辜先生气得脸色发青,他很大的眼睛突出来了,一两分钟说不出话,最后站起来拿手敲着讲台说道:"我当年连袁世凯都不怕,我还怕你?"这件故事,现在想起来还觉很有趣味。辜先生有一次谈到在袁世凯时代他不得已担任了袁世凯为准备帝制而设立的参政院的议员(辜先生虽是帝制派,但他主张的帝制是满清的帝制,不是袁世凯的帝制)。有一天他从会场上出来,收到 300 银元的出席费,他立刻拿了这大包现款到八大胡同去逛窑子。北平当时妓院的规矩,是唱名使妓女鱼贯而过,任狎妓者挑选其所看上的。辜先生到每个妓院点一次名,每个妓女给一块大洋,到 300 块大洋花完了,乃哈哈大笑,扬长而去。

当时在他们旧式社会里,逛妓院与娶姨太太并不认为是不正当的事,所以辜先生还有一个日本籍的姨太太。他是公开主张多妻主义的,他一个最出名的笑话就是:"人家家里只有一个茶壶配上几个茶杯,哪有一个茶杯配上几个茶壶的道理?"这个譬喻早已传诵一时,但其本质确是一种诡辩。不料以后还有因此而连带发生的一个引伸的譬喻。陆小曼同徐志摩结婚以后,她怕徐志摩再同别人谈恋爱,所以对志摩说:"志摩! 你不能拿辜先生茶壶的譬喻来作借口,你要知道,你不是我的茶壶,乃是我的牙刷,茶壶可以公开用的,牙刷是不能公开用的!"作文和说理用譬喻在逻辑上是犯大忌的,因为譬喻常常用性质不同的事物作比,并在这里面隐藏着许多遁词。

辜先生英文写作的特长，就是作深刻的讽刺。我在国外时，看见一本英文杂志里有他的一篇文章，所采的体裁是欧洲中世纪基督教常用的问答传习体(Catechism)。其中有几条我至今还记得很清楚，如："什么是天堂？天堂是在上海静安寺路最舒适的洋房里！谁是傻瓜？傻瓜是任何外国人在上海不能发财的！什么是侮辱上帝？侮辱上帝是说赫德(Sir Robert Hart)总税务司为中国定下的海关制度并非至善至美。"诸如此类的问题有二三十个，用字和造句的深刻和巧妙，真是可以令人拍案叫绝。大约是在1920年美国《纽约时报》的星期杂志上有一篇辜先生的论文，占满第一页全面。中间插入一个辜先生的漫画像，穿着前清的顶戴朝服，后面拖了一根大辫子。这篇文章的题目是"没有文化的美国"(The Uncivilized United States)。他批评美国文学的时候说美国除了 Edgar Allan Poe 所著的 Annabelle Lee 之外，没有一首好诗。诸如此类的议论很多，可是美国这个权威的大报，却有这种幽默感把他全文登出。美国人倒是有种雅量，欢喜人家骂他，愈骂得痛快，他愈觉得舒服，只要你骂的技术够巧妙。像英国的王尔德、萧伯纳都是用这一套方法得到美国人的崇拜。在庚子八国联军的时候，辜先生曾用拉丁文在欧洲发表一篇替中国说话的文章，使欧洲人士大为惊奇。善于运用中国的观点来批评西洋的社会和文化，能够搔着人家的痒处，这是辜先生能够得到西洋文艺界赞美佩服的一个理由。

无疑义的，辜先生是一个有天才的文学家，常常自己觉得怀才不遇，所以搞到恃才傲物。他因为生长在华侨社会之中，而华侨常饱受着外国人的歧视，所以他对外国人自不免取嬉笑怒骂的态度以发泄此种不平之气。他又生在中国混乱的社会里，更不免愤世嫉俗。他走到旧复辟派这条路上去，亦是不免故意好奇立异，表示与众不同。他曾经在教室里对我们说过："现在中国只有两个好人，一个是蔡元培先生，一个是我。因为蔡先生点了翰林之后不肯做官就去革命，到现在还是革命。我呢？自从跟张文襄(之洞)做了前清的官以后，到现在还是保皇。"这可能亦是他自己的解嘲和答客难吧！

PREFACE

THE object of this book is an attempt to interpret the spirit and show the value of the Chinese civilisation. Now in order to estimate the value of a civilisation, it seems to me, the question we must finally ask is not what great cities, what magnificent houses, what fine roads it has built and is able to build; what beautiful and comfortable furniture, what clever and useful implements, tools and instruments it has made and is able to make; no, not even what institutions, what arts and sciences it has invented: the question we must ask, in order to estimate the value of a civilisation,—is, *what type of humanity*, what kind of men and women it has been able to produce. In fact, the man and woman,—the type of human beings—which a civilisation produces, it is this which shows the essence, the personality, so to speak, the soul of that civilisation. Now if the men and women of a civilisation show the essence, the personality and soul of that civilisation, the language which a man and woman speak, shows the essence, the personality, the soul of the man and woman. The French say of literary composition, "*Le style, c'est l'homme.*" I have therefore taken these three things, the Real Chinaman, the Chinese woman and the Chinese language,—as the subjects of the first three essays in this volume to illustrate the spirit and show the value of the Chinese civilisation.

I have added to these, two essays in which I have tried to show how and why men, foreigners who are looked upon as authorities on the subject, do not really understand the real Chinaman and the Chinese language. The Rev. Arthur Smith, who wrote the Chinese

5

Characteristics, I have tried to show, does not understand the real Chinaman, because, being an American, —he is not deep enough to understand the real Chinaman. Dr. Giles again, who is considered a great sinologue, I have tried to show, does not really understand the Chinese language, because, being an Englishman, he is not broad enough, —he has not the philosophic insight and the broadness which that insight gives, I have wanted to include in this volume and essay I wrote on J. B. Bland and Backhouse's book on the famous late Empress Dowager, but unfortunately I have not been able to find a copy of that essay which was published in the "National Review" in Shanghai some four years ago. In that essay, I have tried to show that, such men as J. B. Bland and Backhouse do not and cannot understand the real Chinese woman, —the highest type of woman produced by the Chinese civilisation viz the late Empress Dowager, because such men as J. B. Bland and Backhouse are not simple, —have not the simplicity of mind, being too clever and having, like all modern men, a distorted intellect. * In fact, in order to understand the real Chinaman and the Chinese civilisation, a man must be deep, broad and simple, for the three characteristics of the Chinese character and the Chinese civilisation are: depth, broadness and simplicity.

The American people, I may be permitted to say here, find it difficult to understand the real Chinaman and the Chinese civilisation, because the American people, as a rule, are broad, simple, but not deep. The English cannot understand the real Chinaman and Chinese civilisation because the English, as a rule, are deep, simple, but not broad. The Germans again cannot understand the real Chinaman and the Chinese civilisation because the Germans, espe-

---

* Mencius says, "What I hate in your clever men is that they always distort things. 所恶于智者为其凿也" Bk IV. Part II. 26.

cially the educated Germans, as a rule, are deep, broad, but not simple. The French, —well the French are the people, it seems to me, who can understand and has understood the real Chinaman and the Chinese civilisation best. * The French, it is true, have not the depth of nature of the Germans nor the broadness of mind of the Americans nor the simplicity of mind of the English, —but the French, the French people have to a preeminent degree a quality of mind such as all the people I have mentioned above as a rule, have not, —a quality of mind which, above all things, is necessary in order to understand the real Chinaman and the Chinese civilisation; a quality of mind viz: *delicacy*, For, in addition to the three characteristics of the real Chinaman and Chinese civilisation which I have already mentioned, I must here add one more, and that the chief characteristic, namely delicacy; delicacy to a preeminent degree such as you will find nowhere else except perhaps among the ancient Greeks and their civilisation.

It will be seen from what I have said above that the American people if they will study the Chinese civilisation, will get depth; the English, broadness; and the Germans, simplicity; and all of them, Americans, English and Germans by the study of the Chinese civilisation, of Chinese books and literature, will get a quality of mind which, I take the liberty of saying here that it seems to me, they all of them, as a rule, have not to a preeminent degree, namely, *delicacy*. The French people finally, by the study of the Chinese civilisation, will get all, —depth, broadness, simplicity and a still finer delicacy than the delicacy which they now have. Thus the study of the Chinese civilisation, of Chinese books and literature will, I believe, be of

---

* The best book written in any European Language on the spirit of the Chinese civilisation is a book called "La Cité Chinoise" by G. —Eug. Simon who was once French Consul in China. It was from this book that Prof. Lowes Dickinson of Cambridge, as he himself told me, drew his inspiration in writing his famous "Letters from John Chinaman."

benefit to all the people of Europe and America. I have therefore added to this volume an essay on Chinese scholarship, —the sketch of a programme how to study Chinese, which I made for myself when I made up my mind and began, after my return from Europe, to study the civilisation of my own country, exactly now thirty years ago; this sketch of a programme how to study Chinese which I hope will be of help to those who want to study Chinese and the Chinese civilisation.

Last of all, I have included as an appendix an essay on practical politics, —an essay on "The War and the Way out." Knowing full well the danger of entering into the arena of practical politics, I nevertheless do it, because in order to prove the value of the Chinese civilisation, I want to show how the study of the Chinese civilisation can help to solve the problem facing the world to-day, —the problem of saving the civilisation of Europe from bankruptcy, In fact I want to show that the study of Chinese, of Chinese books and Chinese literature is not only a hobby for sinologues.

In this essay, I have tried to show the moral causes which have brought on this war; for until the true moral causes of this war are understood and remedied, there can be no hope of finding a way out of it. The moral causes of this war, I have tried in my essay to show, are the *worship of the mob* in Great Britain and the *worship of might* in Germany. I have, in my essay, laid emphasis more upon the worship of the mob in Great Britain, than the worship of might in Germany, because looking impartially upon the question, it seems to me that it is the worship of the mob in Great Britain, which is responsible for the worship of might in Germany; in fact, the worship of the mob in all European countries and especially in Great Britain, it was this which has created the enormous German Millitarism which everybody now hates and denounces.

Now let me first of all say here that it is the *moral fibre* in the

German nation, their intense love of righteousness and, as a consequence, their equally intense hatred of unrighteousness, hatred of all
untidiness and disorder (Unzucht und Unordnung), which makes the
German people believe in and worship might. All men who intensely
love righteousness, who intensely hate unrighteousness are inclined to
believe in and worship might. The Scotch Carlyle, for instance, believed in and worshipped might. Why? Because Carlyle with the German moral fibre in him intensely hated unrighteousness. Now the
reason why I say that it is the worship of the mob in Great Britain
which is responsible for the worship of might in Germany, is because,
the *moral fibre*—the intense hatred of unrighteousness, of untidiness
and disorder in the German nation makes them hate the mob, the
worship of the mob and the mob worshippers in Great Britain. After
the German nation saw how the mob and the mob-worshipping politi-
cians of Great Britain made the Boer War in Africa, their *instinctive*
intense hatred * for the mob, the mob-worship and the mob-worshippers in Great Britain made the German nation willing to make heavy
sacrifices, made the *whole German nation ready to starve themselves
to create a Navy* with the hope to put down the mob, the mob-worship and the mob-worshippers in Great Britain. In fact, the German
nation, I may say, found themselves surrounded on all sides by the
mob, mob-worship and mobworshippers encouraged by Great Britain
in all Europe and this made the German nation believe more and more
in might, made the German nation worship might as the only salvation for mankind. This worship of might in Germany created by the
hatred for the Religion of mob worship in Great Britain, thus created
the enormous monstrous German Militarism which everybody now

---

* The famous telegram of the German Emperor to President Kruger was an *instinctive*
outsburst of indignation of the true Gernamic soul with its moral fibre against Joseph Cham-
berlain and his Cockney class in England, who manipulated the Boer War.

hates and denounces.

Thus, I say again, it is the worship of the mob, the Religion of the worship of the mob in all European countries, especially in Great Britain, which is responsible for the worship of might in Germany; which has created the abnormal enormity and monstrosity of German Militarism in Europe to-day. If therefore the people in Great Britain and the people in all European countries and America want to put down German Militarism, —they must try first to put down the mob, the mob-worshippers and the Religion of mob-worship in their own countries. * To the people of Europe and America, and in Japan and China too, to-day who speak of and want liberty, I will venture here to say that the only way, it seems to me, to get liberty, true liberty is to behave themselves; to learn to behave themselves properly. Look at China before this Revolution. There was more liberty among the Chinese people, —no priest, no policeman, no Municipal tax, no income tax to bother them—more liberty among the Chinese than among any other people in the world; and why? Because the Chinese people before this Revolution behaved themselves; knew how to behave themselves; knew how to behave themselves as *good citizens*. But now after this Revolution—there is less liberty in China, and why? Because the modern queueless, up-to-date Chinamen, the returned students have learnt from the people of Europe and America, —learnt from the European mob in Shanghai how to *misbehave themselves*; to behave themselves not as good citizens, but as a *mob*—a mob encouraged, coddled and worshipped by the British

---

* Confucius said to a disciple "when outside nations are dissatisfied with you, you should cultivate *civil* or *Civic* virtues (远人不服则修文德)." The British aristocracy, however, like the Manchu aristocracy in China, are now helpless against the mob and mob worshippers in England. But it is, I must say, a great credit to the British aristocracy that not one of them as far as I know, has joined the mob in England in their shout, howl and yell in this war.

10

diplomats and the British Inspector General of Customs in Peking. *
In fact, what I want to say here is, that if the people in Europe, the
people in Great Britain want to put down German Militarism, Prussian Militarism, they must keep the mob in their own countries in order; they must make the mob in their own countries behave themselves properly; in fact they must put down the Religion of mob-worship, and the mob-worshippers in their own countries.

But now while I say that the British people with their mob worship
and encouragement of mob-worship are responsible for the worship of
might in Germany, for German Militarism, I must at the same time say
here that, looking again impartially upon the question, it seems to me that
the *direct* responsibility for this war rests more heavily upon the German
people, upon the German nation, than upon anybody else.

In order to understand this, let me first of all here give the history of German Militarism in Europe. After the Reformation and the
Thirty Years War, the Germanic nations, the people of the Germanic
race with their *moral fibre*, with their intense love of righteousness
and their intense hatred of unrighteousness, hatred of all untidiness
and disorder, the German people, with Militarism as a sword in their
hand, became the rightful guardian of civilisation in Europe. In other
words, the responsibility for putting order and tidiness (Zucht und
Ordnung) in Europe; in fact, the *moral hegemony* so to speak of
Europe came into the hands of the German people. After the Reformation, Frederick the Great, like Cromwell in England, had to take

* To show what a mob the Chinese returned students have become, I may mention here
that some of these students in Peking last year actually wrote letters to the "Peking Gazette,"
a newspaper conducted by a clever Chinese "Babu" by the name of Eugene Chen, openly
threatening to organise and carry out a public assault upon me for criticising the new Chinese
woman in my essay on "the Chinese woman." This clever Chinese "Babu" Eugene Chen the
instigator of the contemplated piece of rowdyism now is a respected member of the Committee
of the Anglo-Chinese Friendship Bureau under the patronage of the British Minister and the
I. G. of the Chinese Customs!

up and use the sword of German Militarism to put order and tidiness in Europe and he succeeded in putting order and tidiness at any rate in the Northern part of Europe. Now see what happened after Frederick the Great's death. His successor did not know how to use the sword of German Militarism in order to guard and protect the civilisation of Europe; in fact, he was unfit to hold the moral hegemony of Europe. The result was, the whole of Europe, even the courts in Germany became a bottomless pit of abominations covered up only with the veneer of civilisation; so much so that at last the suffering population, the plain men and women in France rose up with pikes to protest against the abominations. The plain men and women in France who rose up to protest against the abominations very soon became a *mob*, and this mob finally found a great and able leader, Napoleon Bonaparte, * who led them to rob, murder, kill and ravage all Europe until the nations in Europe rallying round the small nucleus of *sound* German Militarism left in Europe, put an end to the career of the great leader of the mob at Waterloo. After this the moral hegemony of Europe should have returned to the people of the Germanic race, to the Prussians, the back bone of the German nations. But the jealousy of the other races which formed the Austrian Empire prevented this. The result was that without the German nation with its moral fibre and the sword of German Militarism to keep down the mob, the mob in 1848 again rose up furiously to break the civilisation, of Europe. Then again the German nation—the backbone of the Germanic nations, the Prussians with their moral fibre and the sword of German Militarism, saved Europe,—saved Kingship, (Bismarck called it the dynasty), saved civilisation in Europe from the mob.

---

* Emerson with great insight, says, "What sent Napoleon to St. Helena, was not loss of battles, but the *parvenu*, the vulgar ambition in him—the vulgar ambition to marry a real Princess, to found a dynasty."

But now the Austrians, —the other races forming the Austrian Empire again became jealous and would not allow the German nation, —the backbone of the Germanic nations, Prussia to take over the moral hegemony of Europe until 1866 when the Prussian King Wilhelm with Bismarck and Moltke had to put down the Austrian jealousy by force and took over the hegemony into their hands. After this, Louis Napoleon, not like his great uncle a leader, but a swindler of the mob or, as Emerson calls him, a successful thief, tried with the mob of Paris behind him, to dispute and wrest the moral hegemony of Europe from the German nation. The result was that the Emperor Wilhelm with the sharp sword of German militarism in his hand had to march to Sedan and put down the poor successful thief and swindler of the mob. The plain men and women of Paris who put their trust in the mob and the swindler of the mob had their houses sacked and burnt *not by the German Militarism*, not by the Germans and Prussians, but by the very mob in whom they put their trust. After 1872, —not only the moral, but the actual political hegemony of Europe passed finally into the hands of the German nation with the moral fibre of the Germanic race in their soul and the sword of German Militarism in their hand, to hold down the mob and keep the peace in Europe and thanks to the moral fibre in the German nation and the sword of German Militarism, Europe since 1872 has now enjoyed peace for 43 years. Thus people who abuse and denounce German Militarism and Prussian Militarism should remember how much Europe owes to this very German, this Prussian Militarism which they now abuse and denounce.

I have in the above taken the trouble to give this rough short sketch of the German Militarism in Europe in order to make the German people see that I am not prejudiced against them in saying what I am going to say to show that the actual *direct* responsibility for this war rests more heavily upon them, upon the German people and German nation than upon anybody else. I say that the actual *direct* responsibility for this war rests more heavily upon the German people and German nation than upon anybody else; and why? —Because *power means responsibility*. *

I say that it is the intense love of righteousness, the intense hatred of unrighteousness, intense hatred of all untidiness and disorder (Unzucht und Unordnung) in the German people which makes them believe in and worship might. Now I want to say here that this hatred of unrighteousness, hatred of untidiness and disorder, when it becomes over-intense, when it is carried to excess becomes also an *unrighteousness*, becomes a frightful and terrible unrighteousness, something more sinful and wrong even than untidiness and disorder. It was this over intense hatred of unrighteousness which came from their intense love of righteousness, the intense, narrow, hard, rigid hatred of unrighteousness carried to excess in the old Hebrew people—the Hebrew people to whom the people of Europe owe their knowledge and love of righteousness, it was this which destroyed the Jewish nation. It was from this over-intense narrow, hard, rigid hatred of unrighteousness that Jesus Christ came to save His people. Christ, with what Matthew Arnold calls his unspeakable sweet reasonableness said to his own people: "Learn of me, that I am *mild* and lowly and yet shall have peace in your souls." But the Jews—his own people would not listen to him; they, instead of listening to him, crucified him and the consequence was—the Jewish nation perished. To the Romans who were then the guardians of civilisation in Europe, Christ said, "All

---

* Confucius says, "Possession of power without leniency and generosity is a thing which I never can bear to see. (居上不宽吾何以观之) Shakespeare says: "Oh, it is glorious to have a giant's strength: but it is tyrannous to use it like a giant."

they that take the sword shall perish with the sword!"* But the Romans would not listen, but instead, all owed the Jews to crucify him. The consquence was—the Roman Empire and the old civilisation of Europe perished and passed away. Goethe says: "What a long way mankind must have travelled before they came to know how to deal gently even with sinners, to be merciful to law-breakers, *and to be human even to the inhuman*. Truly they were men of Divine nature who first taught this and who gave their lives for it in order to make the realisation of this possible and to hasten the practice of it. "(Welchen Weg musste nicht die Menschheit machen, bis sie dahin gelangte, auch gegen Seluldige gelind, gegen Verbrecher schonend, gegen auch Unmenschliche menschlich zu sein. Gewiss waren as Manner göttlicher Natur, die dies zuerst lehrten, die ihr Leben damit zubrachten, die Ausübung möglich zu machen und zu beschleunigen.)"

With those words of their great Goethe I will endure here to appeal to the German people, to the German nation and say to them that, unless they find a way to put down their narrow, hard, rigid, excessive hatred of unrighteousness which makes them believe so absolutely in and worship might, unless they put away their absolute belief in and worship of might—they, the German nation, like the Jewish nation, will perish and what is more, the modern civilisation of Europe for want of a strong guardian, will collapse and pass away just as the ancient civilisation of Europe passed away. For it is this over-intense, narrow hard, rigid hatred of unrighteousness which makes the German people, the German nation believe in and worship might; and it is this absolute belief in and worship of might which makes the German nation, the German diplomats, German officials and the Ger-

---

* That is to say, all who depend and put their faith solely upon material brute force or as Emerson says, who believe in the vulgar musket worship.

man people so inconsiderate and tactless in their behaviour towards other people. When my German friends have asked me to show them a proof of the German worship of might, of German tactlessness, I have simply pointed the Kettler memorial in Peking to them. The Kettler memorial in Peking is a standing monument of the German worship of might, of the tactlessness of the German diplomacy, thetactlessness of the German nation in their international dealings with other nations. * It was this worship of might of the German nation, this tactlessness of the German diplomacy of which the Kettler memorial is a standing monument, which made the Emperor of Russia say: "We have stood this for seven years; now it must finish;" this tactlessness of the German diplomacy which made the really peaceloving Emperor of Russia and the best people in Europe, the soundest, most loveable, kindest and most generous-hearted people in Europe the Russians take the side of the mob and mob-worshippers in Great Britain and in France, which created the Triple-Entente; which made the Russians finally take the side even of the anarchic mob in Servia and thus brought on this war. In one word it is this tactlessness of the German diplomacy, of the German people, of the German nation which is *directly* reponsible for this war.

I say therefore, if the German nation at this moment the true, rightful and legitimate guardian of the modern civilisation of Europe to-day, is not to perish and the modern European civilisation is to be saved, —the German nation, the German people must find a way to

---

* The German Minister Baron Kettler during the fanatic Boxer outbreak in China was accidentally killed by a madman from the fanatic soldiery. As a punishment for this act of a mad man, the German diplomats insisted upon branding the whole Chinese nation on the forehead with an indelible mark of humiliation, by having this Kettler memorial erected in the principal street of the Chinese Capital. See note on Page 12. The late Count Cassini, Russian Minister in Peking just before the Boxer outbreak, said in an interview with an American journalist, "The Chinese are a *polite people*, but the impoliteness of the British and German Ministers, —especially of the German Minister in Peking is something outrageous."

put down their over-intense, narrow, hard, rigid hatred of unrighteousness which makes them believe so absolutely in and worship might; in fact they must find a way to put down their absolute belief in and worship of might which makes them so inconsiderate and tactless. But then, where are the German nation, the German people to find a way to put down their absolute belief in and worship of might? The German nation, the German people, I say, will find this in these words of their great Goethe. Goethe says: "*There are two peaceful powers in this world : Right and Tact.*" (Es gibt zwei friedliche Gewalten auf der Welt: Das Recht und die Schicklichkeit.)

Now this Right and Tact, *das Recht und die Schicklichkeit*, is the essence of the Religion of good citizenship which Confucius gave to us Chinese here in China; this Tact, this *Schicklichkeit*, especially, is the essence of the Chinese civilisation. The Religion in the civilisation of the Hebrew people taught the people of Europe the knowledge of Right, but it did not teach Tact. The civilisation of Greece taught the people of Europe the knowledge of Tact but it did not teach Right. But the Religion in the civilisation of China teaches us Chinese both Right and Tact, —das Recht und die Schicklichkeit. The Hebrew Bible, the plan of civilisation according to which the people of Europe have built their present modern civilisation, teaches the people of Europe to love righteousness, to be righteous men, to do right. But the Chinese Bible—the Five Canons and Four Books in China, the plan of civilisation which Confucius saved for us the Chinese nation, teaches us Chinese also to love righteousness; to be righteous men; to do right, but it adds: "Love righteousness, be righteous men, do right—but *with good taste*." In short, Religion in Europe says: "Be a good man." But the Religion in China says: "Be a good man *with good taste*." Christianity sys: "Love Mankind." But Confucius says: "Love Mankind *with good taste*." This Religion of

17

righteousness with good taste, which I have called the Religion of good citizenship, is the new religion I believe, which the people of Europe, especially the people of the countries now at war, want at this moment not only to put an end to this war, but to save the civilisation of Europe, to save the civilisation of the world. This new Religion, the people of Europe will find here in China, —in the Chinese civilisation. I have therefore in this little book made the attempt to interpret and show the value of this, —the Chinese civilisation. I do this with the hope that all educated serious thinking people, who read this book of mine will, by reading this book, better understand the moral causes of this war and understanding the moral causes of this war, will all help to put an end to this cruel, inhuman, useless and most monstrous war which the world has ever seen.

Now if we want to help to put an end to this war, we must, all of us, try to put down first the worship of the mob and then the worship of might in the world to-day, which, as I have said, are the cause of this war. We can put down the worship of the mob, only when in our daily life, in everything we say and do, every one of us will think, not of interests, of expediency—*of what will pay*, but think of that word in Goethe's saying—*Right*. Confucius says: "The gentleman understands *right*; the *cad* understands *interests*,—*what will pay*." Further we can only put down the worship of the mob in the world when we have the courage, even if it does not pay to do so, to refuse to join and go in with the crowd—with the *mob*. Voltaire says: "C'est le malheur des gens honnêtes qu'ils sont des laches. It is the misfortune of so-called good people that they are cowards." For it is the selfishness and cowardice in all of us, I want to say here, selfishness which makes us think of interests, of expediency, of what will pay, instead of right, and cowardice which makes us afraid to stand up alone against the crowd, against the mob, —it is

18

this selfishness and cowardice in all of us which has given rise and created the mob and the worship of the mob in the world to-day. People say German Militarism is the enemy and danger of the world to-day. But I say it is the selfishness and cowardice in all of us which is the real enemy of the world to-day: selfishness and cowardice in all of us, which, when combined, becomes Commercialism. It is this spirit of Commercialism, in all countries of the world, especially in Great Britain and America, which is the real enemy of the world to-day. It is, I say, this spirit of Commercialism in all of us and not Prussian Militarism which is the real, the greatest enemy of the world to-day. For it is this Commercialism, a combination of selfishness and cowardice which has created the Religion of the worship of the mob and it is this Religion of the worship of the mob in Great Britain which has created the Religion of the worship of might in Germany, created the German Militarism which, as I said, finally brought on this war. *The fons et origo* of this war, I say, therefore is not militarism, but *Commercialism*, which, as I said, is a combination of selfishness and cowardice in all of us. Thus, if we want to help to put an end to this war, we must, all of us, first put down the spirit of Commercialism, the combination of selfishness and cowardice in us; in short, we must first of all, think of *right* and not of interests and then have the courage to stand up against the crowd, against the mob. In this way, I say, and *only in this way* we can help to put down the worship of the mob, the Religion of the worship of the mob and in putting down this worship of the mob, this Religion of the worship of the mob, we can help to put an end to this war.

Now as soon as we have put down the worship of the mob, it will then be very easy to put down the worship of might, easy to put down German Militarism, put down Prussian Militarism. The only thing we will have to do, in order to put down the worship of might, to put down German, Prussian or any Militarism in the world, is to think of the other word in that saying of Goethe—*Schicklichkeit*, *Tact*, *Good Taste* and, in thinking of that, to behave with tact and good taste, in short to behave properly; for might, Militarism, even Prussian Militarism can do nothing and will soon find itself useless and unnescessary against people who know how to behave themselves properly. This then is the essence of the Religion of good citizenship; this is the secret of the Chinese civilisation. This is also the secret of the new civilisation of Europe which the German Goethe gave to the people of Europe and the secret of this civilisation is: to put down force, *not* by force, but by *right and tact*; in fact to put down force and everything that is evil in this world, not by force, but by ordering our conversation aright and behaving ourselves properly; and ordering our conversation aright and behaving properly means *to do right and to behave with tact and good taste*. * This is the secret, the soul of the Chinese civilisation, the essence of the spirit of the Chinese people, which I have tried in this book to interpret and explain.

Finally I will here conclude with the words with which I concluded the book "Papers from a Viceroy's Yamen" which I wrote after the Boxer trouble in China. They are the words of the French poet Béranger and I think they are very appropriate at the present moment.

J' ai vu la Paix descendre sur la terre,
Semant de l' or des fleurs et des épis;
L' air était calme et du Dieu de la guerre
Elle étouffait les foudres assoupis.

---

* Confucius says, "The moral man, the gentleman by living a life of simple truth and earnestness can bring peace to the world (君子笃恭而天下平)."

Ah! disait-elle, egaux par la vaillance.
Anglais, Français, Belge, Russe ou Germain,
Peuples, formez une sainte alliance
Et donnez vous la main! *

KU HUNG-MING
Peking, 20th April, 1915.

---

* 我目睹和平徐徐降临，
　她把金色的花朵麦穗撒遍大地：
　战争的硝烟已经散尽
　她抑制了使人昏厥的战争霾雾。
　啊！她说，同样都是好汉，
　英法比俄德人
　去结成一个神圣同盟
　拉起你的手吧！　　——据黄兴涛译文，下同。编者注。

CONTENTS

INTRODUCTION

The Religion of Good-citizenship

Sage, thun wir nicht recht? Wir müssen den Pöbel betrügen,
  Sieh nur, wie ungeschickt, sich nur wie wild er sich zeigt!
Ungeschick und wild sind alle rohen Betrogenen;
  *Seid nur redlich und führt ihn zum Menschlichen an. ***

Goethe

THE great war at the present moment is absorbing all the attention of the world exclusive of everything else. But then I think
this war itself must make serious thinking people turn their attention
to the great problem of civilisation. All civilisation begins by the conquest of Nature, i. e. by subduing and controlling the terrific physical
forces in Nature so that they can do no harm to men. The modern
civilisation of Europe to-day has succeeded in the conquest of Nature
with a success, it must be admitted, hitherto not attained by any other
civilisation. But there is in this world a force more terrible even than
the terrific physical forces in Nature and that is the passions in the
heart of man. The harm which the physical forces of Nature can do to
mankind, is nothing compared with the harm which human passions
can do. Until therefore this terrible force, —the human passions—is
properly regulated and controlled, there can be, it is evident, not only
no civilisation, but even no life possible for human beings.

In the first early and rude stage of society, mankind had to use

---

* Aren't we just doing the right thing? the mob we must befool them;
   See, now, how shiftless! and look now how wild! for such is the mob.
  Shiftless and wild all sons of Adam are when you befool them;
   Be but honest and true, and thus make human, them all.

physical force to subdue and subjugate human passions. Thus hordes of savages had to be subjugated by sheer physical force. But as civilisation advances, mankind discovers a force more potent and more effective for subduing and controlling human passions than physical force and this force is called *moral force*. The moral force which in the past has been effective in subduing and controlling the human passions in the population of Europe, is Christianity. But now this war with the armament preceding it, seems to show that Christianity has become ineffective as a moral force. Without an effective moral force to control and restrain human passions, the people of Europe have had again to employ physical force to keep civil order. As Carlyle truly says, "Europe is Anarchy plus a constable." The use of physical force to maintain civil order leads to militarism. In fact militarism is necessary in Europe to-day because of the want of an effective moral force. But militarism leads to war and war means destruction and waste. Thus the people of Europe are on the horns of a dilemma. If they do away with militarism, anarchy will destroy their civilisation, but if they keep up militarism, their civilisation will collapse through the waste and destruction of war. But Englishmen say that they are determined to put down Prussian militarism and Lord Kitchner believes that he will be able to stamp out Prussian militarism with three million drilled and armed Englishmen. But then it seems to me when Prussian militarism is thus stamped out, there will then arise another militarism, —the British militarism which again will have to be stamped out. Thus there seems to be no way of escape out of this vicious circle.

But is there really no way of escape? Yes, I believe there is. The American Emerson long ago said, "I can easily see the bankruptcy of the vulgar musket worship, —though great men be musket worshippers; and 'tis certain, as God liveth, the gun that does need another gun, the law of love and justice alone can effect a clean revolution." Now if the people of Europe really want to put down militarism, there is only one way of doing it and that is, to use what Emerson calls the gun that does not need another gun, the law of love and justice, —in fact, moral force, With an effective moral force, militarism will become unnecesary and disappear of itself. But now, that Christianity has become ineffective as a moral force the problem is where are the people of Europe to find this new effective moral force which will make militarism unnecessary?

I believe the people of Europe will find this new moral force in China, —in the Chinese civilisation. The moral force in the Chinese civilisation which can make militarism unnecessary is the Religion of good citizenship. But people will say to me, "There have also been wars in China." It is true there have been wars in China; but, since the time of Confucius 2, 500 years ago, we Chinese have had no militarism such as that we see in Europe to-day. In China war is an accident, whereas in Europe war has become a necessity. We Chinese are liable to have wars, but we do not live in constant expectation of war. In fact the one thing intolerable in the state of Europe, it seems to me, is not so much war as the fact that every body is constantly afraid that his neighbour as soon as he gets strong enough to be able to do it, will come to rob and murder him and he has therefore to arm himself or pay for an armed policeman to protect him. Thus what weighs upon the people of Europe is not so much the accident of War, but the constant necessity to arm themselves, the absolute neccessity to use physical force to protect themselves.

Now in China because we Chinese have the Religion of good citizenship a man does not feel the need of using physical force to protect himself; he has seldom the need even to call in and use the physical force of the policeman, of the State to protect him. A man in China is protected by the sense of justice of his neighbour; he is protected by the readiness of his fellow men to obey the sense of moral obliga-

4

tion. In fact, a man in China does not feel the need of using physical force to protect himself because he is sure that right and justice is recognised by every body as a force higher than physical force and moral obligation is recognised by every body as something which must be obeyed. Now if you can get all mankind to agree to recognise right and justice, as a force higher than physical force, and moral obligation as something which must be obeyed, then the use of physical force will become unnecessary; then there will be no militarism in the world. But of course there will be in every country a few people, criminals, and in the world, a few savages who will not or are not able to recognise right and justice as a force higher than physical force and moral obligation as something which must be obeyed. Thus against criminals and savages a certain amount of physical or police force and militarism will always be necessary in every country and in the world.

But people will say to me how are you to make mankind recognise right and justice as a force higher than physical force. I answer the first thing you will have to do is to convince mankind of the efficacy of right and justice, convince them that right and justice is a power; in fact, convince them of the *power of goodness*. But then again how are you to do this? Well, —in order to do this, the Religion of good citizenship in China teaches every child as soon as he is able to understand the meaning of words, that *the Nature of man is good*. *

Now the fundamental unsoundness of the civilisation of Europe to-day, it seems to me, lies in its wrong conception of human nature; its conception that human nature is evil and because of this wrong conception, the whole structure of society in Europe has always rest-

---

* The first sentence of the first book that is put into the hands of every child in China when he goes to school

ed upon force. The two things which the people of Europe have depended upon to maintain civil order are Religion and Law. In other words, the population of Europe have been kept in order by the fear of God and the fear of the Law. Fear implies the use of force. Therefore in order to keep up the fear of God, the people of Europe had at first to maintain a large number of expensive idle persons called *priests*. That, to speak of nothing else, meant so much expense, that it at last became an unbearable burden upon the people. In fact in the thirty years war of the Reformation, the people of Europe tried to get rid of the priest. After having got rid of the priests who kept the population in order by the fear of God, the people of Europe tried to maintain civil order by the fear of the Law. But to keep up the fear of the Law, the people of Europe have had to maintain another class of still more expensive idle persons called *policemen and soldiers*. Now the people of Europe are beginning to find out that the maintainence of policemen and soldiers to keep civil order, is still more ruinously expensive than even the maintainence of priests. In fact, as in the thirty years war of the Reformation, the people of Europe wanted to get rid of the priest, so in this present war, what the people of Europe really want, is to get rid of the soldier. But the alternatives before the people of Europe if they want to get rid of the policeman and soldier, is either to call back the priest to keep up the fear of God or to find something else which, like the fear of God and the fear of the Law, will help them to maintain civil order. That, to put the question broadly, I think, everybody will admit, is the great problem of civilisation before the people of Europe after this war.

Now after the experience which they have had with the priests, I do not think the people of Europe will want to call back the priests. Bismarck has said, "We will never go back to Canossa." Besides, even if the priests are now called back, they would be useless, for the fear of God is gone from the people of Europe. The only other alternative before the people of Europe therefore, if they want to get rid of the policeman and soldier, is to find something else, which, like the fear of God and the fear of the Law, can help them to maintain civil order. Now this something, I believe, as I have said, the people of Europe will find in the Chinese civilisation. This something is what I have called the Religion of good citizenship. This Religion of good citizenship in China is a religion which can keep the population of a country in order without priest and without policeman or soldier. In fact with this Religion of good citizenship, the population of China, a population as large, if not larger than the whole population of the Continent of Europe, are actually and practically kept in peace and order without priest and without policeman or soldier. In China, as every one who has been in this country knows, the priest and the policeman or soldier, play a very subordinate, a very insignificant part in helping to maintain public order. Only the most ignorant class in China require the priest and only the worst, .the criminal class in China, require the policeman or soldier to keep them in order. Thus I say if the people of Europe really want to get rid of Religion and Militarism, of the priest and soldier which have caused them so much trouble and bloodshed, they will have to come to China to get this, what I have called the Religion of good citizenship.

In short what I want to call the attention of the people of Europe and America to, just at this moment when civilisation seems to be threatened with bankruptcy, is that there is an invaluable and hitherto unsuspected asset of civilisation here in China. The asset of civilisation is not the trade, the railway, the mineral wealth, gold, silver, iron or coal in this country. The asset of civilisation of the world to-day, I want to say here, is the Chinaman, — *the unspoilt real Chinaman* with his Religion of good citizenship. The real Chinaman, I say, is an invaluable asset of civilisation, because *he is a person who costs the world little or nothing to keep him in order*. Indeed I would like here to warn the people of Europe and America not to destroy this invaluable asset of civilisation, not to change and spoil the real Chinaman as they are now trying to do with their New Learning. If the people of Europe and America succeed in destroying the real Chinaman, the Chinese type of humanity; succeed in transforming the real Chinaman into a European or American, i. e., to say, a person who will require a priest or soldier to keep him in order, then surely they will increase the burden either of Religion or of Militarism of the world, —this last item at this moment already becoming a danger and menace to civilisation and humanity. But on the other hand, suppose one could by some means or other change the European or American type of humanity, transform the European or American into a real Chinaman who will then not require a priest or soldier to keep him in order, —just think what a burden will be taken off from the world.

But now to sum up in a few plain words the great problem of civilisation in Europe arising out of this war. The people of Europe, I say, at first tried to maintain civil order by the help of the priest. But after a while, the priest cost too much expense and trouble. The people of Europe then, after the thirty years war, sent away the priest and called in the policeman and soldier to maintain civil order. But now they find the policeman and soldier are causing more expense and trouble even than the priests. Now what are the people of Europe to do? Send away the soldier and call back the priest? No, I do not believe the people of Europe will want to call back the priest. Besides the priest now would be useless. But then what are the people of Europe to do? I see Professor Lowes Dickinson of Cambridge in an article in the Atlantic Monthly, entitled "The War and the Way out," says: "Call in the *mob*." I am afraid the mob when once called in to take the place of the priest and soldier, will give more trouble than even the priest and the soldier. The priests and soldiers in Europe have caused wars, but the mob will bring revolution and anarchy and then the state of Europe will be worse than before. Now my advice to the people of Europe is: Do not call back the priest, and for goodness sake don't call in the mob, —but call in the Chinaman; *call in the real Chinaman with his Religion of good citizenship and his experience of 2,500 years how to live in peace without priest and without soldier*.

In fact I really believe that the people of Europe will find the solution of the great problem of civilisation after this war, —here in China. There is, I say here again, an invaluable, but hitherto unsuspected asset of civilisation here in China, and the asset of civilisation is the real Chinaman. The real Chinaman is an asset of civilisation because he has the secret of a new civilisation which the people of Europe will want after this great war, and the secret of that new civilisation is what I have called the Religion of good citizenship. The first principle of this Religion of good citizenship is to believe that the *Nature of Man is good*; to believe in the power of goodness; to believe in the power and efficacy of what the American Emerson calls the law of love and justice. But what is the law of love? The Religion of good citizenship teaches that the law of love means to *love your father and mother*. And what is the law of justice? The Religion of good citizenship teaches that the law of justice means to be true, to be faithful, to be loyal; that the woman in every country must be selflessly, absolutely loyal to her husband, that the man in every country must be selflessly, *absolutely loyal to his sovereign*, to his King or Emperor. In fact the highest duty in this Religion of good citizenship I want to say finally here is the *Duty of Loyalty*, loyalty not only in deed, but loyalty in spirit or as Tennyson puts it,

> *To reverence the King as he were*
> *Their conscience and their conscience as their King,*
> *To break the heathen and uphold the Christ.*

THE SPIRIT OF THE CHINESE PEOPLE

A Paper that was to have been read before the Oriental
Society of Peking

LET me first of all explain to you what I propose, with your permission, this afternoon to discuss. The subject of our paper I
have called "The Spirit of the Chinese people." I do not mean here
merely to speak of the character or characteristics of the Chinese people. Chinese characteristics have often been described before, but I
think you will agree with me that such description or enumeration of
the characteristics of the Chinese people hitherto have given us no
picture at all of the inner being of the Chinaman. Besides, when we
speak of the character or characteristics of the Chinese, it is not possible to generalize. The character of the Northern Chinese, as you
know, is as different from that of the Southern Chinese as the character of the Germans is different from that of the Italians.

But what I mean by the spirit of the Chinese people, is the spirit
by which the Chinese people live, something constitutionally distinctive in the mind, temper and sentiment of the Chinese people which
distinguishes them from all other people, especially from those of
modern Europe and America. Perhaps I can best express what I mean
by calling the subject of our discussion the Chinese type of humanity,
or, to put it in plainer and shorter words, the real Chinaman.

Now, what is the real Chinaman? That, I am sure, you will all
agree with me, is a very interesting subject, especially at the present
moment, when from what we see going on around us in China to-
day, it would seem that the Chinese type of humanity—the real Chinaman—is going to disappear and, in his place, we are going to have

a new type of humanity—the progressive or modern Chinaman. In fact I propose that before the real Chinaman, the old Chinese type of humanity, disappears altogether from the world we should take a good last look at him and see if we can find anything organically distinctive in him which makes him so different from all other people and from the new type of humanity which we see rising up in China today.

Now the first thing, I think, which will strike you in the old Chinese type of humanity is that there is nothing wild, savage or ferocious in him. Using a term which is applied to animals, we may say of the real Chinaman that he is a domesticated creature. Take a man of the lowest class of the population in China and, I think, you will agree with me that there is less of animality in him, less of the wild animal, of what the Germans call *Rohheit*, than you will find in a man of the same class in a European society. In fact, the one word, it seems to me, which will sum up the impression which the Chinese type of humanity makes upon you is the English word "gentle." By gentleness I do not mean softness of nature or weak submissiveness. "The docility of the Chinese," says the late Dr. D. J. Macgowan, "is not the docility of a broken-hearted, emasculated people." But by the word "gentle" I mean absence of hardness, harshness, roughness, or violence, in fact of anything which jars upon you. There is in the true Chinese type of humanity an air, so to speak, of a quiet, sober, chastened mellowness, such as you find in a piece of well-tempered metal. Indeed the very physical and moral imperfections of a real Chinaman are, if not redeemed, at least softened by this quality of gentleness in him. The real Chinaman may be coarse, but there is no grossness in his coarseness. The real Chinaman may be ugly, but there is no hideousness in his ugliness. The real Chinaman may be vulgar, but there is no aggressiveness, no blatancy in his vulgarity. The real Chinaman may be stupid, but there is no absurdity in his stupidity. The real Chinaman may be cunning, but there is no deep malignity in his cunning. In fact what I want to say is, that even in the faults and blemishes of body, mind and character of the real Chinaman, there is nothing which revolts you. It is seldom that you will find a real Chinaman of the old school, even of the lowest type, who is positively repulsive.

I say that the total impression which the Chinese type of humanity makes upon you is that he is gentle, that he is inexpressibly gentle. When you analyse this quality of inexpressible gentleness in the real Chinaman, you will find that it is the the product of a combination of two things, namely, sympathy and intelligence. I have compared the Chinese type of humanity to a domesticated animal. Now what is that which makes a domesticated animal so different from a wild animal? It is something in the domesticated animal which we recognise as distinctively human. But what is distinctively human as distinguished from what is animal? It is intelligence. But the intelligence of a domesticated animal is not a thinking intelligence. It is not an intelligence which comes to him from reasoning. Neither does it come to him from instinct, such as the intelligence of the fox, — the vulpine intelligence which knows where eatable chickens are to be found. This intelligence which comes from instinct, of the fox, all, — even wild, animals have. But this, what may be called *human* intelligence of a domesticated animal is something quite different from the vulpine or animal intelligence. This intelligence of a domesticated animal is an intelligence which comes not from reasoning nor from instinct, but from sympathy, from a feeling of love and attachment. A thorough-bred Arab horse understands his English master not because he has studied English grammar nor because he has an instinct for the English language, but because he loves and is attached to his master. This is what I call human intelligence, as distinguished from mere vulpine or animal intelligence. It is the possession of this human quality which distinguishes domesticated from wild animals. In the same way, I say, it is the possession of this sympathetic and true human intelligence, which gives to the Chinese type of humanity, to the real Chinaman, his inexpressible gentleness.

I once read somewhere a statement made by a foreigner who had lived in both countries, that the longer a foreigner lives in Japan the more he dislikes the Japanese, whereas the longer a foreigner lives in China the more he likes the Chinese. I do not know if what is said of the Japanese here, is true. But, I think, all of you who have lived in China will agree with me that what is here said of the Chinese is true. It is well-known fact that the liking—you may call it the taste for the Chinese—grows upon the foreigner the longer he lives in this country. There is an indescribable something in the Chinese people which, in spite of their want of habits of cleanliness and refinement, in spite of their many defects of mind and character, makes foreigners like them as foreigners like no other people. This indescribable something which I have defined as gentleness, softens and mitigates, if it does not redeem, the physical and moral defects of the Chinese in the hearts of foreigners. This gentleness again is, as I have tried to show you, the product of what I call sympathetic or true human intelligence—an intelligence which comes not from reasoning nor from instinct, but from sympathy—from the power of sympathy. Now what is the secret of the power of sympathy of the Chinese people?

I will here venture to give you an explanation—a hypothesis, if you like to call it so—of the secret of this power of sympathy in the Chinese people and my explanation is this. The Chinese people have this power, this strong power of sympathy, because they live wholly, or almost wholly, a life of the heart. The whole life of Chinaman is a life of feeling—not feeling in the sense of sensation which comes from the bodily organs, nor feeling in the sense of passions which flow, as you would say, from the nervous system, but feeling in the sense of emotion or *human affection* which comes from the deepest part of our nature—the heart or soul. Indeed I may say here that the real Chinaman lives so much a life of emotion or human affection, a life of the soul, that he may be said sometimes to neglect more than he ought to do, even the necessary requirements of the life of the senses of a man living in this world composed of body and soul. That is the true explanation of the insensibility of the Chinese to the physical discomforts of unclean surroundings and want of refinement. But that is neither here nor there.

The Chinese people, I say, have the power of sympathy because they live wholly a life of the heart—a life of emotion or human affection. Let me here, first of all, give you two illustrations of what I mean by living a life of the heart. My first illustration is this. Some of you may have personally known an old friend and colleague of mine in Wuchang—known him when he was Minister of the Foreign Office here in Peking—Mr. Liang Tun-yen, Mr. Liang told me, when he first received the appointment of the Customs Taotai of Hankow, that what made him wish and strive to become a great mandarin, to wear the red button, and what gave him pleasure then in receiving this appointment, was not because he cared for the red button, not because he would henceforth be rich and independent, —and we were all of us very poor then in Wuchang, —but because he wanted to rejoice, because this promotion and advancement of his would gladden the heart of his old mother in Canton. That is what I mean when I say that the Chinese people live a life of the heart—a life of emotion or human affection.

My other illustration is this. A Scotch friend of mine in the Customs told me he once had a Chinese servant who was a perfect scamp, who lied, who "squeezed," and who was always gambling, but when my friend fell ill with typhoid fever in an out-of-the-way port where he had no foreign friend to attend to him, this awful scamp of a Chinese servant nursed him with a care and devotion which he could not have expected from an intimate friend or near relation. Indeed I think what was once said of a woman in the Bible may also be said, not only of the Chinese servant, but of the Chinese people generally:—"Much is forgiven them, because they love much." The eyes and understanding of the foreigner in China see many defects and blemishes in the habits and in the character of the Chinese, but his heart is attracted to them, because the Chinese have a heart, or, as I said, live a life of the heart—a life of emotion or human affection.

Now we have got, I think, a clue to the secret of sympathy in the Chinese people—the power of sympathy which gives to the real Chinaman that sympathetic or true human intelligence, making him so inexpressibly gentle. Let us next put this clue or hypothesis to the test. Let us see whether with this clue that the Chinese people live a life of the heart we can explain not only detached facts such as the two illustrations I have given above, but also general characteristics which we see in the actual life of the Chinese people.

First of all let us take the Chinese language. As the Chinese live a life of the heart, the Chinese language, I say, is also a language of the heart. Now it is a well-known fact that children and uneducated persons among foreigners in China learn Chinese very easily, much more so than grown-up and educated persons. What is the reason of this? The reason, I say, is because children and uneducated persons think and speak with the language of the heart, whereas educated men, especially men with the modern intellectual education of Europe, think and speak with the language of the head or intellect. In fact, the reason why educated foreigners find it so difficult to learn Chinese, is because they are too educated, too intellectually and scientifically educated. As it is said of the Kingdom of Heaven, so it may also be said of the Chinese language:—"Unless you become as little children, you cannot learn it."

Next let us take another well-known fact in the life of the Chinese people. The Chinese, it is well-known, have wonderful memories. What is the secret of this? The secret is: the Chinese remember things with the heart and not with the head. The heart with its power of sympathy, acting as glue, can retain things much better than the head or intellect which is hard and dry. It is, for instance, also for this reason that we; all of us, can remember things which we learnt when we were children much better than we can remember things which we learnt in mature life. As children, like the Chinese, we remember things with the heart and not with the head.

Let us next take another generally admitted fact in the life of the Chinese people—their politeness. The Chinese are, it has often been remarked, a peculiarly polite people. Now what is the essence of true politeness? It is consideration for the feelings of others. The Chinese are polite because, living a life of the heart, they know their own feelings and that makes it easy for them to show consideration for the feelings of others. The politeness of the Chinese, although not elaborate like the politeness of the Japanese, is pleasing because it is, as the French beautifully express it, *la politesse du coeur*, the politeness of the heart. The politeness of the Japanese, on the other hand, although elaborate, is not so pleasing, and I have heard some foreigners express their dislike of it, because it is what may be called a rehearsal politeness—a politeness learnt by heart as in a theatrical piece. It is not a spontaneous politeness which comes direct from the heart. In fact the politeness of the Japanese is like a flower without fragrance, whereas the politeness of a really polite Chinese has a perfume like the aroma of a precious ointment—*instar unguenti fragrantis*— which comes from the heart.

Last of all, let us take another characteristic of the Chinese people, by calling attention to which the Rev. Arthur Smith has made his reputation, viz.:—want of exactness. Now what is the reason for this want of exactness in the ways of the Chinese people? The reason, I say again, is because the Chinese live a life of the heart. The heart is a very delicate and sensitive balance. It is not like the head or intellect, a hard, stiff, rigid instrument. You cannot with the heart think with the same steadiness, with the same rigid exactness as you can with the head or intellect. At least, it is extremely difficult to do so. In fact, the Chinese pen or pencil which is a soft brush, may be taken as a symbol of the Chinese mind. It is very difficult to write or draw with it, but when you have once mastered the use of it, you will, with it, write and draw with a beauty and grace which you cannot do with a hard steel pen.

Now the above are a few simple facts connected with the life of the Chinese people which anyone, even without any knowledge of Chinese, can observe and understand, and by examining these facts, I think, I have made good my hypothesis that the Chinese people live a life of the heart.

Now it is because the Chinese live a life of the heart, the life of a child, that they are so primitive in many of their ways. Indeed, it is a remarkable fact that for a people who have lived so long in the world as a great nation, the Chinese people should to this day be so primitive in many of their ways. It is this fact which has made superficial foreign students of China think that the Chinese have made no progress in their civilisation and that the Chinese civilisation is a stagnant one. Nevertheless, it must be admitted that, as far as pure intellectual life goes, the Chinese are, to a certain extent, a people of arrested development. The Chinese, as you all know, have made little or no progress not only in the physical, but also in the pure abstract sciences such as mathematics, logic and metaphysics. Indeed the very words "science" and "logic" in the European languages have no exact equivalent in the Chinese language. The Chinese, like children who live a life of the heart, have no taste for the abstract sciences, because in these the heart and feelings are not engaged. In fact, for everything which does not engage the heart and feelings, such as tables of statistics, the Chinese have a dislike amounting to aversion. But if tables of statistics and the pure abstract sciences fill the Chinese with aversion, the physical sciences as they are now pursued in Europe, which require you to cut up and mutilate the body of a living animal in order to verify a scientific theory, would inspire the Chinese with repugnance and horror.

The Chinese, I say, as far as pure intellectual life goes, are to a certain extent, a people of arrested development. The Chinese to this day live the life of a child, a life of the heart. In this respect, the Chinese people, old as they are as a nation, are to the present day, a nation of children. But then it is important you should remember that this nation of children, who live a life of the heart, who are so primitive in many of their ways, have yet a *power of mind and rationality* which you do not find in a primitive people, a power of mind and rationality which has enabled them to deal with the complex and difficult problems of social life, government and civilisation with a success which, I will venture to say here, the ancient and modern nations of Europe have not been able to attain—a success so signal that they have been able practically and actually to keep in peace and order a greater portion of the population of the Continent of Asia under a great Empire.

In fact, what I want to say here, is that the wonderful peculiarity of the Chinese people is not that they live a life of the heart. All primitive people also live a life of the heart. The Christian people of medieval Europe, as we know, also lived a life of the heart. Matthew Arnold says:—"The poetry of medieval Christainity lived by the heart and imagination." But the wonderful peculiarity of the Chinese people, I want to say here, is that, while living a life of the heart, the life of a child, they yet have a power of mind and rationality which you do not find in the Christian people of medieval Europe or in any other primitive people. In other words, the wonderful peculiarity of the Chinese is that for a people, who have lived so long as a grown-up nation, as a nation of adult reason, they are yet able to this day to live the life of a child—a life of the heart.

Instead, therefore, of saying that the Chinese are a people of arrested development, one ought rather to say that the Chinese are a people who never grow old. In short the wonderful peculiarity of the Chinese people as a race, is that they possess the secret of perpetual youth.

Now we can answer the question which we asked in the beginning:—What is the real Chinaman? The real Chinaman, we see now, is a man who lives the life of a man of adult reason with the heart of a child. In short the real Chinaman is a person *with the head of a grown-up man and the heart of a child*. The Chinese spirit, therefore, is a spirit of perpetual youth, the spirit of national immortality. Now what is the secret of this national immortality in the Chinese people? You will remember that in the beginning of this discussion I said that what gives to the Chinese type of humanity—to the real Chinaman—his inexpressible gentleness is the possession of what I called sympathetic or true human intelligence. This true human intelligence, I said, is the product of a combination of two things, sympathy and intelligence. It is a working together in harmony of the heart and head. In short it is a happy union of soul with intellect. Now if the spirit of the Chinese people is a spirit of perpetual youth, the spirit of national immortality, the secret of this immortality is this happy union of soul with intellect.

You will now ask me where and how did the Chinese people get this secret of national immortality—this happy union of soul with intellect, which has enabled them as a race and nation to live a life of perpetual youth? The answer, of course, is that they got it from their civilisation. Now you will not expect me to give you a lecture on Chinese civilisation within the time at my disposal. But I will try to tell you something of the Chinese civilisation which has a bearing on our present subject of discussion.

Let me first of all tell you that there is, it seems to me, one great fundamental difference between the Chinese civilisation and the civilisation of modern Europ. Here let me quote an admirable saying of a famous living art critic, Mr. Bernard Berenson. Comparing European with Oriental art, Mr. Berenson says: — "Our European art has the fatal tendency to become science and we hardly possess a masterpiece which does not bear the marks of having heen *a battlefield for divided interests*." Now what I want to say of the European civilisation is that it is, as Mr. Berenson says of European art, a battlefield for divided interests; a continuous warfare for the divided interests of science and art on the one hand, and of religion and philosophy on the other; in fact a terrible battlefield where the head and the heart—the soul and the intellect—come into constant conflict. In the Chinese civilisation, at least for the last 2,400 years, there is no such conflict. That, I say, is the one great fundamental difference between the Chinese civilisation and that of modern Europe.

In other words, what I want to say, is that in modern Europe, the people have a religion which satisfies their heart, but not their head, and a philosophy which satisfies their head but not their heart. Now let us look at China. Some people say that the Chinese have no religion. It is certainly true that in China even the mass of the people do not take seriously to religion. I mean religion in the European sense of the word. The temples, rites and ceremonies of Taoism and Buddhism in China are more objects of recreation than of edification; they touch the aesthetic sense, so to speak, of the Chinese people rather than their moral or religious sense; in fact, they appeal more to their imagination than to their heart or soul. But instead of saying that the Chinese have no religion, it is perhaps more correct to say that the Chinese do not want—do not feel the need of religion.

Now what is the explanation of this extraordinary fact that the Chinese people, even the mass of the population in China, do not feel the need of religion? It is thus given by an Englishman. Sir Robert K. Douglas, Professor of Chinese in the London University, in his study of Confucianism, says:—"Upwards of forty generations of Chinamen have been absolutely subjected to the dicta of one man. Being a Chinaman of Chinamen the teachings of Confucius were specially suited to the nature of those he taught. *The Mongolian mind being eminently phlegmatic and unspeculative*, naturally rebels against the idea of investigating matters beyond its experiences. With the idea of a future life still unawakened, a plain, matter-of-fact system of morality, such as that enunciated by Confucius, was sufficient for all the wants of the Chinese."

That learned English professor is right, when he says that the Chinese people do not feel the need of religion, because they have the teachings of Confucius, but he is altogether wrong, when he asserts that the Chinese people do not feel the need of religion because the Mongolian mind is phlegmatic and unspeculative. In the first place religion is not a matter of speculation. Religion is a matter of feeling, of emotion; it is something which has to do with the human soul. The wild, savage man of Africa even, as soon as he emerges from a mere animal life and what is called the soul in him, is awakened, — feels the need of religion. Therefore although the Mongolian mind may be phlegmatic and unspeculative, the Mongolian Chinaman, who, I think it must be admitted, is a higher type of man than the wild man of Africa, also has a soul, and, having a soul, must feel the need of religion unless he has something which can take for him the place of religion.

The truth of the matter is, —the reason why the Chinese people do not feel the need of religion is because they have in Confucianism a system of philosophy and ethics, a synthesis of human society and civilisation which can take the place of religion. People say that Confucianism is not a religion. It is perfectly true that Confucianism is not a religion in the ordinary European sense of the word. But then I say the greatness of Confucianism lies even in *this*, that it is *not* a religion. In fact, the greatness of Confucianism is that, without being a religion, it can take the place of religion; it can make men do without religion.

Now in order to understand how Confucianism can take the place of religion we must try and find out the reason why mankind, why men feel the need of religion. Mankind, it seems to me, feel the need of religion for the same reason that they feel the need of science, of art and of philosophy. The reason is because man is a being who has a soul. Now let us take science, I mean physical science. What is the reason which makes men take up the study of science? Most people now think that men do so, because they want to have railways and aeroplanes. But the motive which impels the true men of science to pursue its study is not because they want to have railways and aeroplanes. Men like the present progressive Chinamen, who take up the study of science, because they want railways and aeroplanes, will never get science. The true men of science in Europe in the past who have worked for the advancement of science and brought about the possibility of building railways and aeroplanes, did not think at all of railways and aeroplanes. What impelled those true men of science in Europe and what made them succeed in their work for the advancement of science, was because they *felt in their souls* the need of understanding the awful mystery of the wonderful universe in which we live. Thus mankind, I say, feel the need of religion for the same reason that they feel the need of science, art and philosophy; and the reason is because man is a being who has a soul, and because the soul in him, which looks into the past and future as well as the present—not like animals which live only in the present—feels the need of understanding the mystery of this universe in which they live. Until men understand something of the nature, law, purpose and aim of the things which they see in the universe, they are like children in a dark room who feel the danger, insecurity and uncertainty of everything. In fact, as an English poet says, the burden of the mystery of the universe weighs upon them. Therefore mankind want science, art and philosophy for the same reason that they want religion, to lighten for them "the burden of the mystery, ...

> The heavy and the weary weight of
> All this unintelligible world."

Art and poetry enable the artist and poet to see beauty and order in the universe and that lightens for them the burden of this mystery. Therefore poets like Goethe, who says: "He who has art, has religion," do not feel the need of religion. Philosophy also enables the philosophers to see method and order in the universe, and that lightens for them the burden of this mystery. Therefore philosophers, like Spinoza, "for whom," it has been said, "the crown of the intellectual life is a transport, as for the saint the crown of the religious life is a transport," do not feel the need of religion. Lastly, science also enables the scientific men to see law and order in the universe, and that lightens for them the burden of this mystery. Therefore scientific men like Darwin and Professor Haeckel do not feel the need of religion.

But for the mass of mankind who are not poets, artists, philosophers or men of science; for the mass of mankind whose lives are full of hardships and who are exposed every moment to the shock of accident from the threatening forces of Nature and the cruel merciless passions of their fellow-men, what is it that can lighten for them the "burden of the mystery of all this unintelligible world?" It is religion. But how does religion lighten for the mass of mankind the burden of this mystery? Religion, I say, lightens this burden by giving the mass of mankind a sense of *security* and a sense of *permanence*. In presence of the threatening forces of Nature and the cruel merciless passions of their fellowmen and the mystery and terror which these inspire, religion gives to the mass of mankind a refuge—a refuge in which they can find a sense of *security*; and that refuge is a belief in some supernatural Being or beings who have absolute power and control over those forces which threaten them. Again, in presence of the constant change, vicissitude and transition of things in their own lives—birth, childhood, youth, old age and death, and the mystery and uncertainty which these inspire, religion gives to the mass of mankind also a refuge—a refuge in which they can find a sense of *permanence*; and that refuge is the belief in a future life. In this way, I say, religion lightens for the mass of mankind who are not poets, artists, philosophers or scientific men, the burden of the mystery of all this unintelligible world, by giving them a sense of security and a sense of permanence in their existence. Christ said: "Peace I give unto you, peace which the world cannot give and which the world cannot take away from you." That is what I mean when I say that religion gives to the mass of mankind a sense of security and a sense of permanence. Therefore, unless you can find something which can give to the mass of mankind the same peace, the same sense of security and of permanence which religion affords them, the mass of mankind will always feel the need of religion.

But I said Confucianism, without being a religion can take the place of religion. Therefore, there must be something in Confucianism which can give to the mass of mankind the same sense of security and permanence which religion affords them. Let us now find out what this something is in Confucianism which can give the same sense of security and sense of permanence that religion gives.

I have often been asked to say what Confucius has done for the Chinese nation. Now I can tell you of many things which I think Confucius has accomplished for the Chinese people. But, as to-day I have not the time, I will only here try to tell you of one principal and most important thing which Confucius has done for the Chinese nation—the one thing he did in his life by which, Confucius himself said, men in after ages would know him, would know what he had done for them. When I have explained to you this one principal thing, you will then understand what that something is in Confucianism which can give to the mass of mankind the same sense of security and sense of permanence which religion affords them. In order to explain this, I must ask you to allow me to go a little more into detail about Confucius and what he did.

Confucius, as some of you may know, lived in what is called a period of expansion in the history of China—a period in which the feudal age had come to an end; in which the feudal, the semi-patriarchal social order and form of government had to be expanded and reconstructed. This great change necessarily brought with it not only confusion in the affairs of the world, but also confusion in men's minds. I have said that in the Chinese civilisation of the last 2, 500 years there is no conflict between the heart and the head. But I must now tell you that in the period of expansion in which Confucius lived there was also in China, as now in Europe, a fearful conflict between the heart and the head. The Chinese people in Confucius's time found themselves with an immense system of institutions, established facts, accredited dogmas, customs, laws—in fact, an immense system of society and civilisation which had come down to them from their venerated ancestors. In this system their life had to be carried forward; yet they began to feel—they had a sense that this system was not of their creation, that it by no means corresponded with the wants of their actual life; that, for them, it was customary, not rational. Now the awakening of this sense in the Chinese people 2,500 years ago was the awakening of what in Europe to-day is called the modern spirit—the spirit of liberalism, the spirit of enquiry, to find out the why and the wherefore of things. This modern spirit in China then, seeing the want of correspondence of the old order of society and civilisation with the wants of their actual life, set itself not only to reconstruct a new order of society and civilisation, but also to find a basis for this new order of society and civilisation. But all the attempts to find a new basis for society and civilisation in China then failed. Some, while they satisfied the head—the intellect of the Chinese people, did not satisfy their heart; others, while they satisfied their heart, did not satisfy their head. Hence arose, as I said, this conflict between the heart and the head in China 2,500 years ago, as we see it now in Europe. This conflict of the heart and head in the new order of society and civilisation which men tried to reconstruct made the Chinese people feel dissatisfied with all civilisation, and in the agony and despair which this dissatisfaction produced, the Chinese people wanted to pull down and destroy all civilisation. Men, like Laotzu, then in China as men like Tolstoy in Europe to-day, seeing the misery and suffering resulting from the conflict between the heart and the head, thought they saw something radically wrong in the very nature and constitution of society and civilisation. Laotzu and Chuang-tzu, the most brilliant of Laotzu's disciples, told the Chinese people to throw away all civilisation. Laotzu said to the people of China: "Leave all that you have and follow me; follow me to the mountains, to the hermit's cell in the mountains, there to live a true life—a life of the heart, a life of immortality."

But Confucius, who also saw the suffering and misery of the then state of society and civilisation, thought he recognised the evil was not in the nature and constitution of society and civilisation, but in the wrong track which society and civilisation had taken, in the wrong basis which men had taken for the foundation of society and civilisation. Confucius told the Chinese people not to throw away their civilisation. Confucius told them that in a true society and true civilisation—in a society and civilisation with a *true* basis men also could live a true life, a life of the heart. In fact, Confucius tried hard all his life to put society and civilisation on the right track; to give it a true basis, and thus prevent the destruction of civilisation. But in the last days of his life, when Confucius saw that he could not prevent the destruction of the Chinese civilisation—what did he do? Well, as an architect who sees his house on fire, burning and falling over his head, and is convinced that he cannot possibly save the building, knows that the only thing for him to do is to save the drawings and plans of the building so that it may afterwards be built again; so Confucius, seeing the inevitable destruction of the building of the Chinese civilisation which he conld not prevent, thought he would save the drawings and plans, and he accordingly saved the drawings and plans of the Chinese civilisation, which are now preserved in the Old Testament of the Chinese Bible—the five Canonical Books known as the *Wu Ching*, five Canons. That, I say, was a great service which Confucius has done for the Chinese nation—he saved the drawings and plans of their civilisation for them.

Confucius, I say, when he saved the drawings and plans of the Chinese civilisation, did a great service for the Chinese nation. But that is not the principal, the greatest service which Confucius has done for the Chinese nation. The greatest service he did was that, in saving the drawings and plans of their civilisation, he made a new synthesis, a new interpretation of the plans of that civilisation, and in that new synthesis he gave the Chinese people the true idea of a State—a true, rational, permanent, absolute basis of a State.

But then Plato and Aristotle in ancient times, and Rousseau and

Herbert Spencer in modern times also made a synthesis of civilisation, and tried to give a true idea of a State. Now what is the difference between the philosophy, the synthesis of civilisation made by the great men of Europe I have mentioned, and the synthesis of civilisation—the system of philosophy and morality now known as Confucianism? The difference, it seems to me, is this. The philosophy of Plato and Aristotle and of Herbert Spencer has not become a religion or the equivalent of a religion, the accepted faith of the masses of a people or nation, whereas Confucianism has become a religion or the equivalent of a religion to even the mass of the population in China. When I say religion here, I mean religion, not in the narrow European sense of the word, but in the broad universal sense. Goethe says:—" *Nur saemtliche Menschen erkennen die Natur ; nur saemtliche Menschen leben das Menschliche* * . Only the mass of mankind know what is real life; only the mass of mankind live a true human life." Now when we speak of religion in its broad universal sense, we mean generally a system of teachings with rules of conduct which, as Goethe says, is accepted as true and binding by the mass of mankind, or at least, by the mass of the population in a people or nation. In this broad and universal sense of the word Christianity and Buddhism are religions. In this broad and universal sense, Confucianism, as you know, has become a religion, as its teachings have been acknowledged to be true and its rules of couduct to be binding by the whole Chinese race and nation, whereas the philosophy of Plato, of Aristotle and of Herbert Spencer has not become a religion even in this broad universal sense. That, I say, is the difference between Confucianism and the philosophy of Plato and Aristotle and of Herbert Spencer—the one has remained a philosophy for the learned, whereas the other has become a religion or the equivalent of a religion

---

* 唯有民众懂得什么是真正的生活,唯有民众过着真正的人的生活。

for the mass of the whole Chinese nation as well as for the learned of China.

In this broad universal sense of the word, I say Confucianism is a religion just as Christianity or Buddhism is a religion. But you will remember I said that Confucianism is not a religion in the European sense of the word. What is then the difference between Confucianism and a religion in the European sense of the word? There is, of course, the difference that the one has a supernatural origin and element in it, whereas the other has not. But besides this difference of supernatural and non-supernatural, there is also another difference between Confucianism and a religion in the European sense of the word such as Christianity and Buddhism, and it is this. A religion in the European sense of the word teaches a man to be a good *man*. But Confucianism does more than this; Confucianism teaches a man to be a good *citizen*. The Christian Catechism asks:—"What is the chief end of *man*?" But the Confucian Catechism asks:—"What is the chief end of a *citizen*?" of man, not in his individual life, but man in his relation with his fellowmen and in his relation to the State? The Christian answers the words of his Catechism by saying: "The chief end of man is to glorify God." The Confucianist answers the words of his Catechism by saying: "The chief end of man is to live as a dutiful son and a good citizen." Tzü Yu, a disciple of Confucius, is quoted in the Sayings and Discourses of Confucius, saying: "A wise man devotes his attention to the foundation of life—the chief end of man. When the foundation is laid, wisdom, religion will come. Now to live as a dutiful son and good citizen, is not that the foundation—the chief end of man as a moral being?" In short, a religion in the European sense of the word makes it its object to transform man into a perfect ideal man by himself, into a saint, a Buddha, an angel, whereas Confucianism limits itself to make man into a good citizen—to live as a dutiful son and a good citizen. In other words, a religion in the European sense of the word says:—"If you want to have religion, you must be a saint, a Buddha, an angel;" whereas Confucianism says:—"If you live as a dutiful son and a good citizen, you *have* religion."

In fact, the real difference between Confucianism and religion in the European sense of the word, such as Christianity or Buddhism, is that the one is a personal religion, or what may be called a Church religion, whereas the other is a social religion, or what may be called a State religion. The greatest service, I say, which Confucius has done for the Chinese nation, is that he gave them a true idea of a State. Now in giving this true idea of a State, Confucius made that idea a religion. In Europe politics is a science, but in China, since, Confucius' time, politics is a religion. In short, the greatest service which Confucius has done for the Chinese nation, I say, is that he gave them a Social or State religion. Confucius taught this State religion in a book which he wrote in the very last days of his life, a book to which he gave the name of *Ch'un Ch'iu* (春秋), Spring and Autumn. Confucius gave the name of Spring and Autumn to this book because the object of the book is to give the real moral causes which govern the rise and fall—the Spring and Autumn of nations. This book might also be called the Latter Day Annals, like the Latter Day Pamphlets of Carlyle. In this book Confucius gave a résumé of the history of a false and decadent state of society and civilisation in which he traced all the suffering and misery of that false and decadent state of society and civilisation to its real cause—to the fact that men had not a true idea of a State; no right conception of the true nature of the duty which they owe to the State, to the head of the State, their ruler and Sovereign. In a way Confucius in this book taught the divine right of kings. Now I know all of you, or at least most of you, do not now believe in the divine right of kings. I will not argue the point with you here. I will only ask you to suspend your judgment until you have heard what I have further to say. In the meantime I will just ask your permission to quote to you here a saying of Carlyle. Carlyle says: "The right of a king to govern us is either a divine right or a diabolic wrong." Now I want you, on this subject of the divine right of kings, to remember and ponder over this saying of Carlyle.

In this book Confucius taught that, as in all the ordinary relations and dealings between men in human society, there is, besides the base motives of interest and of fear, a higher and nobler motive to influence them in their conduct, a higher and nobler motive which rises above all considerations of interest and fear, the motive called *Duty*; so in this important relation of all in human society, the relation between the people of a State or nation and the Head of that State or nation, there is also this higher and nobler motive of Duty which should influence and inspire them in their conduct. Bnt what is the rational basis of this duty which the people in a State or nation owe to the head of the State or nation? Now in the feudal age before Confucius' time, with its semi-patriarchal order of Society and form of Government, when the State was more or less a family, the poeple did not feel so much the need of having a clear and firm basis for the duty which they owe to the Head of the State, because, as they were all members of one clan or family, the tie of kinship or natural affection already, in a way, bound them to the Head of the State, who was also the senior member of their clan or family. But in Confucius' time the feudal age, as I said, had come to an end; when the State had outgrown the family, when the citizens of a State were no longer composed of the members of a clan or family. It was, therefore, then necessary to find a new, clear, rational and firm basis for the duty which the people in a State or nation owe to the Head of the State— their ruler and sovereign. Now what new basis did Confucius find for this duty? Confucius found the new basis for this duty in the word *Honour*.

When I was in Japan last year the ex-Minister of Education, Baron Kikuchi, asked me to translate four Chinese characters taken from the book in which, as I said, Confucius taught this State religion of his. The four characters were *Ming fen ta yi* (名分大义). I translated them as the Great Principle of Honour and Duty. It is for this reason that the Chinese make a special distinction between Confucianism and all other religions by calling the system of teaching taught by Confucius not a *chiao* (教)—the general term in Chinese for religion with which they designate other religions, such as Buddhism, Mohammedanism and Christianity—but the *ming chiao* (名教)—the religion of Honour. Again the term *chum tzu chih tao* (君子之道) in the teachings of Confucius, translated by Dr. Legge as "the way of the superior man," for which the nearest equivalent in the European languages is moral law—means literally, the way—*the Law of the Gentleman*. In fact, the whole system of philosophy and morality taught by Confucius may be summed up in one word: the Law of the Gentleman. Now Confucius codified this law of the gentleman and made it a Religion,—a State religion. The first Article of Faith in this State Religion is *Ming fen ta yi*—the Principle of Honour and Duty—which may thus be called: A Code of Honour.

In this State religion Confucius taught that the only true, rational, permanent and absolute basis, not only of a State, but of all Society and civilisation, is this law of the gentleman, the sense of honour in man. Now you, all of you, even those who believe that there is no morality in politics—all of you, I think, know and will admit the importance of this sense of honour in men in human society. But I am not quite sure that all of you are aware of the *absolute* necessity of this sense of honour in men for the carrying on of every form of human society; in fact, as the proverb which says: "There must be honour even among thieves," show—even for the carrying on of a society of thieves. Without the sense of honour in men, all society and civilisation would on the instant break down and become impossible. Will you allow me to show you how this is so? Let us take, for example, such a trivial matter as gambling in social life. Now unless men when they sit down to gamble all recognise and feel themselves bound by the sense of honour to pay when a certain colour of cards or dice turns up, gambling would on the instant become impossible. The merchants again—unless merchants recognise and feel themselves bound by the sense of honour to fulfil their contracts, all trading would become impossible. But you will say that the merchant who repudiates his contract can be taken to the law-court. True, but if there were no law-courts, what then? Besides, the law-court—how can the law-court make the defaulting merchant fulfil his contract? By force. In fact, without the sense of honour in men, society can only be held together for a time by force. But then I think I can show you that force alone cannot hold society permanently together. The policeman who compels the merchant to fulfil his contract, uses force. But the lawyer, magistrate or president of a republic—how does he make the policeman do his duty? You know he cannot do it by force; but then by what? Either by the sense of honour in the policemen or by *fraud*.

In modern times all over the world to-day—and I am sorry to say now also in China—the lawyer, politician, magistrate and president of a republic make the policeman do his duty by fraud. In modern times the lawyer, politician, magistrate and president of a republic tell the policeman that he must do his duty, because it is for the good of society and for the good of his country; and that the good of society means that he, the policeman, can get his pay regularly, without which he and his family would die of starvation. The lawyer, politician or president of a republic who tells the policeman this, I say, uses *fraud*. I say it is fraud, because the good of the country, which for the policeman means fifteen shillings a week, which barely keeps him and his family from starvation, means for the lawyer, politician, magistrate and president of a republic ten to twenty thousand pounds a year, with a fine house, electric light, motor cars and all the comforts and luxuries which the life blood labour of ten thousands of men has to supply him. I say it is fraud because without the recognition of a sense of honour—the sense of honour which makes the gambler pay the last penny in his pocket to the player who wins from him, *without this sense of honour*, all transfer and possession of property which makes the inequality of the rich and poor in society, as well as the transfer of money on a gambling table, has no justification whatever and no binding force. Thus the lawyer, politician, magistrate or president of a republic, although they talk of the good of society and the good of the country, really depend upon the policeman's unconscious sense of honour which not only makes him do his duty, but also makes him respect the right of property and be satisfied with fifteen shillings a week, while the lawyer, politician and president of a republic receive an income of twenty thousand pounds a year. I, therefore, say it is fraud because while they thus demand the sense of honour from the policeman; they, the lawyer, politician, magistrate and president of a republic in modern society believe, openly say and act on the principle that there is no morality, no sense of honour in politics.

You will remember what Carlyle, I told you, said—that the right of a king to govern us is either a divine right or a diabolic wrong. Now this fraud of the modern lawyer, politician, magistrate and president of a republic is what Carlyle calls a diabolic wrong. It is this fraud, this Jesuitism of the public men in modern society, who say and act on the principle that there is no morality, no sense of honour in politics and yet plausibly talk of the good of society and the good of the country; it is this Jesuitism which, as Carlyle says, gives rise to "the widespread suffering, mutiny, delirium, the hot rage of sansculottic insurrections, the cold rage of resuscitated tyrannies, brutal degradation of the millions, the pampered frivolity of the units" which we see in modern society to-day. In short, it is this combination of fraud and force, Jesuitism and Militarism, lawyer and policeman, which has produced Anarchists and Anarchism in modern society, this combination of force and fraud outraging the moral sense in man and producing madness which makes the Anarchist throw bomb and dynamite against the lawyer, politician, magistrate and president of a republic.

In fact, a society without the sense of honour in men, and without morality in its politics, cannot, I say, be held together, or at any rate, cannot last. For in such a society the policeman, upon whom the lawyer, politician, magistrate and president of a republic depend to carry out their fraud, will thus argue with himself. He is told that he must do his duty for the good of society. But he, the poor policeman, is also a part of that society—to himself and his family, at least, the most important part of that society. Now if by some other way than by being a policeman, perhaps by being an anti-policeman, he can get better pay to improve the condition of himself and his family, that also means the good of society. In that way the policeman must sooner or later come to the conclusion that, as there is no such thing as a sense of honour and morality in politics, there is then no earthly reason why, if he can get better pay, which means also the good of society—no reason why, instead of being a policeman, he should not become a revolutionist or anarchist. In a society when the policeman once comes to the conclusion that there is no reason why, if he can get better pay, he should not become a revolutionist or anarchist—that society is doomed. Mencius said:—"When Confucius completed his Spring and Autumn Annals"—the book in which he taught the State religion of his and in which he showed that the society of his time—in which there was then, as in the world to-day, no sense of honour in public men and no morality in politics—was doomed; when Confucius wrote that book, "the Jesuits and anarchists (lit. bandits) of his time, became afraid." (乱臣贼子惧) *

But to return from the digression, I say, a society without the sense of honour cannot be held together, cannot last. For if, as we have seen, even in the relation between men connected with matters of little or no vital importance such as gambling and trading in human society, the recognition of the sense of honour is so important and necessary, how much more so it must be in the relations between men in human society, which establish the two most essential institutions in that society, the Family and the State. Now, as you all know, the rise of civil society in the history of all nations begins always with the institution of marriage. The Church religion in Europe makes marriage a *sacrament*, *i.e.*, something sacred and inviolable. The sanction for the sacrament of marriage in Europe is given by the Church and the authority for the sanction is God. But that is only an outward, formal, or so to speak, legal sanction. The true, inner, the really binding sanction for the inviolability of marriage—as we see it in countries where there is no church religion, is the sense of honour, the law of the gentleman in the man and woman. Confucius says, "The recognition of the law of the gentleman begins with the recognition of the relation between husband and wife."*** In other words, the recognition of the sense of honour—the law of the gentleman—in all countries where there is civil society, establishes the institution of marriage. The institution of marriage establishes the *Family*.

I said that the State religion which Confucius taught is a Code of Honour, and I told you that Confucius made this Code out of the law

---

* Mencius Bk. III, Part II IX, II.
** 中庸—The Universal order XII 4.

of the gentleman. But now I must tell you that long before Confucius' time there existed already in China an undefined and unwritten code of the law of the gentleman. This undefined and unwritten code of the law of the gentleman in China before Confucius' time was known as *li* (礼) the law of propriety, good taste or good manners. Later on in history before Confucius' time a great statesman arose in China—the man known as the great Law-giver of China, generally spoken of as the Duke of Chou (周公) (B. C. 1135)—who first defined, fixed, and made a written code of the law of the gentleman, known then in China as *li*, the law of propriety, good taste or good manners. This first written code of the gentleman in China, made by the Duke of Chou, became known as *Chou li*—the laws of good manners of the Duke of Chou. This Code of the laws of good manners of the Duke of Chou may be consideral as the pre-Confucian religion in China, or, as the Mosaic law of the Jewish nation before Christianity is called, the Religion of the Old Dispensation of the Chinese people. It was this religion of the old dispensation—the first written code of the law of the gentleman called the Laws of good manners of the Duke of Chou—which first gave the sanction for the sacrament and inviolability of marriage in China. The Chinese to this day therefore speak of the sacrament of marriage as *Chou Kung Chih Li* (周公之礼)—the law of good manners of the Duke of Chou. By the institution of the sacrament of marriage, the pre-Confucian or Religion of the Old Dispensation in China established the Family. It secured once for all the stability and permanence of the family in China. This pre-Confucian or Religion of the Old Dispensation known as the laws of good manners of the Duke of Chou in China might thus be called a *Family* religion as distinguished from the *State* religion which Confucius afterwards taught.

Now Confucius in the State religion which he taught, gave a new Dispensation, so to speak, to what I have called the Family religion which existed before his time. In other words, Confucius gave a new, wider and more comprehensive application to the law of the gentleman in the State religion which he taught; and as the Family religion, or Religion of the Old Dispensation in China before his time instituted the sacrament of marriage, Confucius, in giving this new, wider, and more comprehensive application to the law of the gentleman in the State religion which he taught, instituted a new sacrament. This new sacrament which Confucius instituted, instead of calling it *li*—the Law of good manners, he called it *ming fen ta yi*, which I have translated as the Great Principle of Honour and Duty or Code of Honour. By the institution of this *ming fen ta yi* or Code of Honour Confucius gave the Chinese people, instead of a Family religion, which they had before—a State religion.

Confucius, in the State religion which he now gave, taught that, as under the old dispensation of what I have called the Family religion before his time, the wife and husband in a family are bound by the sacrament of marriage, called *Chou Kung Chih Li*, the Law of good manners of the Duke of Chou—to hold their contract of marriage inviolable and to absolutely abide by it, so under the new dispensation of the State religion which he now gave, the people and their sovereign in every State, the Chinese people and their Emperor in China, are bound by this new sacrament called *ming fen ta yi*— the Great Principle of Honour and Duty or Code of Honour established by this State religion—to hold the contract of allegiance between them as something sacred and inviolable and absolutely to abide by it. In short, this new sacrament called *ming fen ta yi*, or Code of Honour which Confucius instituted, is a Sacrament of the Contract of Allegiance, as the old sacrament called *Chou Kung Chih Li*, the Law of Good Manners of the Duke of Chou which was instituted before his time, is a sacrament of marriage. In this way Confucius, as I said, gave a new, wider, and more comprehensive application to the law of the gentleman, and thus gave a new dispensation to what I have called the Family religion in China before his time, and made it a State religion.

In other words, this State religion of Confucius makes a sacrament of the contract of allegiance as the Family Religion in China before his time, makes a sacrament of the contract of marriage. As by the sacrament of marriage established by the Family Religion the wife is bound to be absolutely loyal to her husband, so by this sacrament of the contract of allegiance called *ming fen ta yi*, or Code of Honour established by the State religion taught by Confucius in China, the people of China are bound to be absolutely loyal to the Emperor. This sacrament of the contract of allegiance in the State religion taught by Confucius in China might thus be called the *Sacrament or Religion of Loyalty*. You will remember what I said to you that Confucius in a way taught the Divine right of kings. But instead of saying that Confucius taught the Divine right of kings I should properly have said that Confucius taught the *Divine duty of Loyalty*. This Divine or absolute duty of loyalty to the Emperor in China which Confucius taught derives its sanction, not as the theory of the Divine right of kings in Europe derives its sanction from the authority of a supernatural Being called God or from some abstruse philosophy, but from the law of the gentleman—the sense of honour in man, the same sense of honour which in all countries makes the wife loyal to her husband. In fact, the absolute duty of loyalty of the Chinese people to the Emperor which Confucius taught, derives its sanction from the same simple sense of honour which makes the merchant keep his word and fulfil his contract, and the gambler play the game and pay his gambling debt.

Now, as what I have called the Family religion, the religion, the religion of the old dispensation in China and the Church religion in all countries, by the institution of the sacrament and inviolability

of marriage establishes the Family, so what I have called the State
religion in China which Confucius taught, by the institution of this
new sacrament of the contract of allegiance, establishes the State. If
you will consider what a great service the man who first instituted the
sacrament and established the inviolability of marriage in the world
has done for humanity and the cause of civilisation, you will then, I
think, understand what a great work this is which Confucius did
when he instituted this new sacrament and established the inviolability of the contract of allegiance. The institution of the sacrament of
marriage secures the stability and permanence of the Family, without
which the human race would become extinct. The institution of this
sacrament of the contract of allegiance secures the stability and permanence of the State, without which human society and civilisation
would all be destroyed and mankind would return to the state of savages or animals. I therefore said to you that the greatest thing which
Confucius has done for the Chinese people is that he gave them the
true idea of a State—a true, rational, permanent, and absolute basis
of a State, and in giving them that, he made it a religion, —a State
religion.

Confucius taught this State religion in a book which, as I told
you, he wrote in the very last days of his life, a book to which he
gave the name of Spring and Autumn. In this book Confucius first
instituted the new sacrament of the contract of allegiance called *ming
fen ta yi*, or the Code of Honour. This sacrament is therefore often
and generally spoken of as *Chun Chiu ming fen ta yi* (春秋名分大
义), or simply *Chun Chiu ta yi*—(春秋大义) *i. e.*, the Great
Principle of Honour and Duty of the Spring and Autumn Annals, or
simply the Great Principle or Code of the Spring and Autumn
Annals. This book in which Confucius taught the Divine duty of loyalty is the Magna Charta of the Chinese nation. It contains the sacred
covenant, the sacred social contract by which Confucius bound the

whole Chinese people and nation to be absolutely loyal to the Emperor, and this covenant or sacrament, this Code of Honour, is the one and only true Constitution not only of the State and Government in China, but also of the Chinese civilisation. Confucius said it is by this book that after ages would know him—know what he had done for the world.

I am afraid I have exhausted your patience in taking such a very long way to come to the point of what I want to say. But now we have got to the point where I last left you. You will remember I said that the reason why the mass of mankind will always feel the need of religion—I mean religion in the European sense of the word—is because religion gives them a refuge, one refuge, the belief in an all powerful Being called God in which they can find a sense of permanence in their existence. But I said that the system of philosophy and morality which Confucius taught, known as Confucianism, can take the place of religion, can make men, even the mass of mankind do without religion. Therefore, there must be, I said, something in Confucianism which can give to men, to the mass of mankind, the same sense of security and sense of permanence which religion gives. Now, I think we have found this something. This something is the *Divine duty of loyalty to the Emperor* taught by Confucius in the State religion which he has given to the Chinese nation.

Now, this absolute Divine duty of loyalty to the Emperor of every man, woman, and child in the whole Chinese Empire gives, as you can understand, in the minds of the Chinese population, an absolute, supreme, transcendent, almighty power to the Emperor; and this belief in the absolute, supreme, transcendent, almighty power of the Emperor it is which gives to the Chinese people, to the mass of the population in China, the same sense of security which the belief in God in religion gives to the mass of mankind in other countries. The belief in the absolute, supreme, transcendent, almighty power of the Emperor also secures in the minds of the Chinese population the absolute stability and permanence of the State. This absolute stability and permanence of the State again secures the infinite continuance and lastingness of society. This infinite continuance and lastingness of society finally secures in the minds of the Chinese population the immortality of the race. Thus it is this belief in the immortality of the race, derived from the belief in the almighty power of the Emperor given to him by the Divine duty of loyalty, which gives to the Chinese people, the mass of the population in China, the same sense of permanence in their existence which the belief in a future life of religion gives to the mass of mankind in other countries.

Again, as the absolute Divine duty of loyalty taught by Confucius secures the immortality of the race in the nation, so the cult of ancestor-worship taught in Confucianism secures the immortality of the race in the family. Indeed, the cult of ancestorworship in China is not founded much on the belief in a future life as in the belief of the immortality of the race. A Chinese, when he dies, is not consoled by the belief that he will live a life hereafter, but by the belief that his children, grandchildren, great-grand-children, all those dearest to him, will remember him, think of him, love him, to the end of time, and in that way, in his imagination, dying, to a Chinese, is like going on a long, long journey, if not with the hope, at least with a great "perhaps" of meeting again. Thus this cult of ancestor-worship, together with the Divine duty of loyalty, in Confucianism gives to the Chinese people the same sense of permanence in their existence while they live and the same consolation when they die which the belief in a future life in religion gives to the mass of mankind in other countries. It is for his reason that the Chinese people attach the same importance to this cult of ancestor-worship as they do to the principle of the Divine duty of loyalty to the Emperor. Mencius said: "Of the three great sins against filial piety the greatest is to have no posterity." Thus the whole system of teaching of Confucius which I have called the State religion in China consists really only of two things, loyalty to the Emperor and filial piety to parents—in Chinese, *Chung Hsiao*. (忠孝) In fact, the three Articles of Faith, called in Chinese the *san kang*(三纲), three cardinal duties in Confucianism or the State religion of China, are, in their order of importance—first, absolute duty of loyalty to the Emperor; second, filial piety and ancestor-worship; third, inviolability of marriage and absolute submission of the wife to the husband. The last two of the three Articles were already in what I have called the Family religion, or religion of the old dispensation in China before Confucius' time; but the first Article—absolute duty of loyalty to the Emperor—was first taught by Confucius and laid down by him in the State religion or religion of the new dispensation which he gave to the Chinese nation. This first Article of Faith—absolute duty of loyalty to the Emperor— in Confucianism takes the place and is the equivalent of the First Article of Faith in all religions—the belief in God. It is because Confucianism has this equivalent for the belief in God of religion that Confucianism, as I have shown you, can take the place of religion, and the Chinese people, even the mass of the population in China, do not feel the need of religion.

But now you will ask me how without a belief in God which religion teaches, how can one make men, make the mass of mankind, follow and obey the moral rule which Confucius teaches, the absolute duty of loyalty to the Emperor, as you can by the authority of God which the belief in God gives, make men follow and obey moral rules given by religion? Before I answer your question, will you allow me first to point out to you a great mistake which people make in believing that it is the sanction given by the authority of God which makes men obey the rules of moral conduct. I told you that the sanction for the sacrament and inviolability of marriage in Europe is given by the

Church, and the authority for the sanction, the Church says, is from God. But I said that was only an outward formal sanction. The real true inner sanction for the inviolability of marriage as we see it in all countries where there is no Church religion, is the sense of honour, the law of the gentleman in the man and woman. Thus the real authority for the obligation to obey rules of moral conduct is the moral sense, the law of the gentleman, in man. The belief in God is, therefore, not necessary to make men obey rules of moral conduct.

It is this fact which has made sceptics like Voltaire and Tom Paine in the last century, and rationalists like Sir Hiram Maxim today, say, that the belief in God is a fraud or imposture invented by the founders of religion and kept up by priests. But that is a gross and preposterous libel. All great men, all men with great intellect, have all always believed in God. Confucius also believed in God, although he seldom spoke of it. Even Napoleon with his great, practical intellect believed in God. As the Psalmist says: "Only the fool—the man with a vulgar and shallow intellect—has said in his heart, ' There is no God. '" But the belief in God of man of great intellect is different from the belief in God of the mass of mankind. The belief in God of men of great intellect is that of Spinoza: a belief in the Divine Order of the Universe. Confucius said: "At fifty I knew the Ordinance of God" * —*i.e.*, the Divine Order of the Universe. Men of great intellect have given different names to this Divine Order of the Universe. The German Fichte calls it the Divine idea of the Universe. In philosophical language in China it is called *Tao*—the Way. But whatever name men of great intellect may give to this Divine Order of the Universe, it is the knowledge of this Divine Order of the Universe which makes men of great intellect see the *absolute* necessity of obeying rules of moral conduct or moral laws which form part of that Divine

---

* 论语—Discourses and Sayings Chap. II 4.

Order of the Universe.

Thus, although the belief in God is not necessary to make men obey the rules of moral conduct, yet the belief in God is necessary to make men see the *absolute* necessity of obeying these rules. It is the knowledge of the absolute necessity of obeying the rules of moral conduct which enables and makes all men of great intellect follow and obey those rules. Confucius says: "A man without a knowledge of the Ordinance of God, *i.e.*, the Divine Order of the Universe, will not be able to be a gentleman or moral man." * But then, the mass of mankind, who have not great intellect, cannot follow the reasoning which leads men of great intellect to the knowledge of the Divine Order of the Universe and cannot therefore understand the absolute necessity of obeying moral laws. Indeed, as Matthew Arnold says: "Moral rules, apprehended as ideas first, and then rigorously followed as laws are and must be for the sage only. The mass of mankind have neither force of intellect enough to apprehend them as ideas nor force of character enough to follow them strictly as laws." It is for this reason that the philosophy and morality taught by Plato, Aristotle and Herbert Spencer have a value only for scholars.

But the value of religion is that it enables men, enables and can make even the mass of mankind who have not force of intellect nor force of character, to strictly follow and obey the rules of moral conduct. But then how and by what means does religion enable and make men do this? People imagine that religion enables and makes men obey the rules of moral conduct by teaching men the belief in God. But that, as I have shown you, is a great mistake. The one and sole authority which makes men really obey moral laws or rules of moral conduct is the moral sense, the law of the gentleman in them. Confucius said: "A moral law which is outside of man is not a moral law."

---

* Discourses and Sayings Chap. XX 3.

Even Christ in teaching His religion says: "The Kingdom of God is within you." I say, therefore, the idea which people have that religion makes men obey the rules of moral conduct by means of teaching them the belief in God is a mistake. Martin Luther says admirably in his commentary on the Book of Daniel: "A God is simply that whereon the human heart *rests* with trust, faith, hope and love. If the resting is right, then the God, too, is right; if the resting is wrong, then the God, too, is illusory." This belief in God taught by religion is, therefore, only a *resting*, or, as I call it, a refuge. But then Luther says: "The resting, *i.e.* the belief in God, must be true, otherwise the resting, the belief, is illusory. In other words, the belief in God must be a true knowledge of God, a real knowledge of the Divine Order of the Universe, which, as we know, only men of great intellect can attain and which the mass of mankind cannot attain. Thus you see the belief in God taught by religion, which people imagine enables the mass of mankind to follow and obey the rules of moral conduct, is illusory. Men rightly call this belief in God—in the Divine Order of the Universe taught by religion—a faith, a trust, or, as I called it, a refuge. Nevertheless, this refuge, the belief in God, taught by religion, although illusory, an illusion, helps towards enabling men to obey the rules of moral conduct, for, as I said, the belief in God gives to men, to the mass of mankind, a sense of security and a sense of permanence in their existence. Goethe says: "Piety, (Frommigkeit) *i.e.*, the belief in God, taught by religion, is not an end in itself but only a means by which, through the complete and perfect calmness of mind and temper (Gemuethsruehe) which it gives, to attain the highest state of culture or human perfection." In other words, the belief in God taught by religion, by giving men a sense of security and a sense of permanence in their existence, calms them, gives them the necessary calmness of mind and temper to feel the law of the gentleman or moral sense in them, which, I say again, is the one and sole authority to make men really obey the rules of moral conduct or moral laws.

But if the belief in God taught by religion only helps to make men obey the rules of moral conduct, what is it then upon which Religion depends principally to make men, to make the mass of mankind, obey the rules of moral conduct? It is *inspiration*. Matthew Arnold truly says: "The noblest souls of whatever creed, the pagan Empedocles as well as the Christian Paul, have insisted on the necessity of inspiration, a living emotion to make moral actions perfect." Now what is this inspiration or living emotion in Religion, the paramount virtue of Religion upon which, as I said, Religion principally depends to make men, to enable and make even the mass of mankind obey the rules of moral conduct or moral laws?

You will remember I told you that the whole system of the teachings of Confucius may be summed up in one word: the Law of the Gentleman, the nearest equivalent for which in the European languages, I said, is moral law. Confucius calls this law of the gentleman a secret. * Confucius says: "The law of the gentleman is to be found everywhere, and yet it is a secret." Nevertheless Confucius says: "The simple intelligence of ordinary men and women of the people even can know something of this secret. The ignoble nature of ordinary men and women of the people, too, can carry out this law of the gentleman." For this reason Goethe, who also knew this secret—the law of the gentleman of Confucius, called it an "open secret." Now where and how did mankind come to discover this secret? Confucuis said, you will remember, I told you that the recognition of the law of the gentleman began with the recognition of the relation of husband and wife—the true relation between a man and woman in marriage. Thus the secret, the open secret of Goethe, the law of the gentleman

---

* 中庸—The Universal order XII 1.

of Confucius, was first discovered by a man and woman. But now, a-
gain, how did the man and the woman discover this secret—the law
of the gentleman of Confucius?

I told you that the nearest equivalent in the European languages
for the law of the gentleman of Confucius, is moral law. Now what is
the difference between the law of the gentleman of Confucius and
moral law—I mean the moral law or law of morality of the philosopher and moralist as distinguished from religion or law of morality
taught by religious teachers. In order to understand this difference
between the law of the gentleman of Confucius and the moral law of
the philosopher and moralist, let us first find out the difference that
there is between religion and the moral law of the philosopher and
moralist. Confucius says: "The Ordinance of God is what we call the
law of our being. To fulfil the law of our being is what we call the
Moral Law. The Moral Law when refined and put into proper order
is what we call Religion." * Thus, according to Confucius, the difference between Religion and moral law—the moral law of the philosopher and moralist—is that Religion is a refined and well ordered
moral law, a deeper or higher standard of moral law.

The moral law of the philosopher tells us we must obey the law
of our being called Reason. But Reason, as it is generally understood,
means our reasoning power, that slow process of mind or intellect
which enables us to distinguish and recognise the definable properties
and qualities of the outward forms of things. Reason, our reasoning
power, therefore, enables us to see in moral relations only the definable properties and qualities, the *mores*, the morality, as it is rightly
called, the outward manner and dead form, the body, so to speak, of
right and wrong, or justice. Reason, our reasoning power alone,
cannot make us see the undefinable, living, absolute essence of right

---

* 中庸 The Universal Order I.1.

and wrong, or justice, the life or soul, so to speak, of justice. For this reason Laotzu says: "The moral law that can be expressed in language is not the absolute moral law. The moral idea that can be defined with words is not the absolute moral idea." * The moral law of the moralist again tells us we must obey the law of our being, called Conscience, *i.e.*, our heart. But then, as the Wise Man in the Hebrew Bible says, there are many devices in a man's heart. Therefore, when we take Conscience, our heart, as the law of our being and obey it, we are liable and apt to obey, not the voice of what I have called the soul of justice, the indefinable absolute essence of justice, but the many devices in a man's heart.

In other words Religion tells us in obeying the law of our being we must obey the *true* law of our being, not the animal or carnal law of our being called by St. Paul the *law of the mind of the flesh*, and very well defined by the famous disciple of Auguste Comte, Monsieur Littre, as the law of self preservation and reproduction; but the true law of our being called by St. Paul the *law of the mind of the Spirit*, and defined by Confucius as the law of the gentleman. In short, this true law of our being, which Religion tells us to obey, is what Christ calls the Kingdom of God within us. Thus we see, as Confucius says, Religion is a refined, spiritualized, well-ordered moral law, a deeper higher standard of moral law than the moral law of the philosopher and moralist. Therefore, Christ said: "Except your righteousness (or morality) exceed the righteousness (or morality) of the Scribes and Pharisees (*i e.*, philosopher and moralist) ye shall in no wise enter into the Kingdom of Heaven."

Now, like Religion, the law of the gentleman of Confucius is also a refined, well-ordered moral law—a deeper higher standard of moral law than the moral law of the philosopher and moralist. The moral

---

* 道可道非常道名可名非常名

law of the philosopher and moralist tells us we must obey the law of our being called by the philosopher, Reason, and by the moralist, Conscience. But, like Religion, the law of the gentleman of Confucius tells us we must obey the *true* law of our being, not the law of being of the average man in the street or of the vulgar and impure person, but the law of being of what Emerson calls "the simplest and purest minds" in the world. In fact, in order to know what the law of being of the gentleman is, we must first *be a gentleman* and have, in the words of Emerson, the simple and pure mind of the gentleman developed in him. For this reason Confucius says: "It is the man that can raise the standard of the moral law, and not the moral law that can raise the standard of the man." *

Nevertheless Confucius says we can know what the law of the gentleman is, if we will study and try to acquire the fine feeling or *good taste* of the gentleman. The word in Chinese *li* (礼) for good taste in the teaching of Confucius has been variously translated as ceremony, propriety, and good manners, but the word means really *good taste*. Now this good taste, the fine feeling and good taste of a gentleman, when applied to moral action, is what, in European language, is called the sense of honour. In fact, the law of the gentleman of Confucius is nothing else but the sense of honour. This sense of honour, called by Confucius the law of the gentleman, is not like the moral law of the philosopher and moralist, a dry, dead knowledge of the form or formula of right and wrong, but like the Righteousness of the Bible in Christianity, an instinctive, living, vivid perception of the indefinable, absolute essence of right and wrong or justice, the life and soul of justice called Honour.

Now, we can answer the question: How did the man and woman who first recognised the relation of husband and wife, discover the se-

---

* 论语—Discourses and Sayings Chap. XV 28.

cret, the secret of Goethe, the law of the gentleman of Confucius? The man and woman who discovered this secret, discovered it because they had the fine feeling, the good taste of the gentleman, called when applied to moral action the sense of honour, which made them see the undefinable, absolute essence of right and wrong or justice, the life and soul of justice called Honour. But then what gave, what inspired the man and woman to have this fine feeling, this good taste or sense of honour which made them see the soul of justice called Honour? This beautiful sentence of Joubert will explain it. Joubert says: "Les hommes no sont justes qu' envers ceux qu' ils aiment. Man cannot be truly just to his neighbour unless he *loves* him." Therefore the inspiration which made the man and woman see what Joubert calls true justice, the soul of justice called Honour, and thus enable them to discover the secret—the open secret of Goethe, the law of the gentleman of Coufucius —is Love—the love between the man and the woman which gave birth, so to speak, to the law of the gentleman; that secret, the possession of which has enabled mankind not only to build up society and civilisation, but also to establish religion—to find God. You can now understand Goethe's confession of faith which he puts into the mouth of Faust, beginning with the words:

> Lifts not the Heaven its dome above?
> Doth not the firm-set Earth beneath us lie?

Now, I told you that it is not the belief in God taught by religion, which makes men obey the rules of moral conduct. What really makes men obey the rules of moral conduct is the law of the gentleman—the Kingdom of Heaven within us—to which religion appeals. Therefore the law of the gentleman is really the life of religion, whereas the belief in God together with the rules of moral conduct which religion teaches, is only the body, so to speak, of religion. But if the life of religion is the law of the gentleman, the *soul* of religion, the source of inspiration in religion, —is Love. This love does not merely mean the love between a man and a woman from whom mankind only first learn to know it. Love includes all true human affection, the feelings of affection between parents and children as well as the emotion of love and kindness, pity, compassion, mercy towards all creatures; in fact, all true human emotions contained in that Chinese word *Jen* (仁), for which the nearest equivalent in the European languages is, in the old dialect of Christianity, godliness, because it is the most godlike quality in man, and in modern dialect, humanity, love of humanity, or, in one word, love. In short, the soul of religion, the source of inspiration in religion is this Chinese word *Jen*, love—or call it by what name you like—which first came into the world as love between a man and a woman. This, then, is the inspiration in religion, the paramount virtue in religion, upon which religion, as I said, depends principally to make men, to enable and make even the mass of mankind obey the rules of moral conduct or moral laws which form part of the Divine Order of the universe. Confucius says: "The law of the gentleman begins with the recognition of husband and wife; but in its utmost reaches, it reigns and rules supreme over heaven and earth—the whole universe."

We have now found the inspiration, the living emotion that is in religion. But this inspiration or living emotion in religion is found not only in religion—I mean Church religion. This inspiration or living emotion is known to everyone who has ever felt an impulse which makes him obey the rules of moral conduct above all considerations of self-interest or fear. In fact, this inspiration or living emotion that is in religion is found in every action of men which is not prompted by the base motive of self-interest or fear, but by the sense of duty and honour. This inspiration or living emotion in religion, I say, is found not only in religion. But the value of religion is that the words of the rules of moral conduct which the founders of all great religions have left behind them have, what the rules of morality of philosophers and moralists have not, this inspiration or living emotion which, as Matthew Arnold says, *lights* up those rules and makes it easy for men to obey them. But this inspiration or living emotion in the words of the rules of conduct of religion again is found not only in religion. All the words of really great men in literature, especially poets, have also this inspiration or living emotion that is in religion. The words of Goethe, for instance, which I have just quoted, have also this inspiration or living emotion. But the words of great men in literature, unfortunately, cannot reach the mass of mankind because all great men in literature speak the language of educated men, which the mass of mankind cannot understand. The founders of all the great religions in the world have this advantage, that they were mostly uneducated men, and, speaking the simple language of uneducated men, can make the mass of mankind understand them. The real value, therefore, of religion, the real value of all the great religions in the world, is that it can convey the inspiration or living emotion which it contains even to the mass of mankind. In order to understand how this inspiration or living emotion came into religion, into all the great religions of the world, let us find out how these religions came into the world.

Now, the founders of all the great religions in the world, as we know, were all of them men of exceptionally or even abnormally strong emotional nature. This abnormally strong emotional nature made them feel intensely the emotion of love or human affection, which, as I have said, is the source of the inspiration in religion, the soul of religion. This intense feeling or emotion of love or human affection enabled them to see what I have called the indefinable, absolute essence of right and wrong or justice, the soul of justice which they called righteousness, and this vivid perception of the absolute essence of justice enabled them to see the unity of the laws of right and wrong or moral laws. As they were men of exceptionally strong emotional nature, they had a powerful imagination, which unconsciously personified this unity of moral laws as an almighty supernatural Being. To this supernatural almighty Being, the personified unity of moral laws of their imagination, they gave the name of God, from whom they also believed that the intense feeling or emotion of love or human affection, which they felt, came. In this way, then, the inspiration or living emotion that is in religion came into religion; the inspiration that lights up the rules of moral conduct of religion and supplies the emotion or motive power needful for carrying the mass of mankind, along the straight and narrow way of moral conduct. But now the value of religion is not only that it has an inspiration or living emotion in its rules of moral conduct which lights up these rules and makes it easy for men to obey them. The value of religion, of all the great religions in the world, is that they have an organisation for awakening, exciting, and kindling the inspiration or living emotion in men necessary to make them obey the rules of moral conduct. This organisation in all the great religions of the world is called the Church.

The Church, many people believe, is founded to teach men the belief in God. But that is a great mistake. It is this great mistake of the Christian Churches in modern times which has made honest men like the late Mr. J. A. Froude feel disgusted with the modern Christian Churches. Mr. Froude says: "Many a hundred sermons have I heard in England on the mysteries of the faith, on the divine mission of the clergy, on apostolic succession, etc., but never one that I can recollect on common honesty, on those primitive commandments, 'Thou shalt not lie' and 'Thou shalt not steal.'" But then, with all deference to Mr. Froude, I think he is also wrong when he says here that the Church, the Christian Church, ought to teach morality. The aim of the establishment of the Church no doubt is to make men moral, to make men obey the rules of moral conduct such as "Thou shalt not lie"and "Thou shalt not steal." But the function, the true function of the Church in all the great religions of the world, is not to teach morality, but to teach *religion*, which, as I have shown you, is not a dead square rule such as "Thou shalt not lie"and"Thou shalt not steal," but an inspiration, a living emotion to make men obey those rules. The true function of the Church, therefore, is not to teach morality, but to *inspire* morality, to inspire men to be moral;in fact, to inspire and fire men with a living emotion which makes them moral. In other words, the Church in all the great religions of the world is an organisation, as I said, for awakening and kindling an inspiration or living emotion in men necessary to make them obey the rules of moral conduct. But how does the Church awaken and kindle this inspiration in men?

Now, as we all know, the founders of all the great religions of the world not only gave an inspiration or living emotion to the rules of moral conduct which they taught, but they also inspired their immediate disciples with a feeling and emotion of unbounded admiration, love, and enthusiasm for their person and character. When the great teachers died, their immediate disciples, in order to keep up the feeling and emotion of unbounded admiration, love, and enthusiasm which they felt for their teacher, founded a Church. That, as we know, was the origin of the Church in all the great religions of the world. The Church thus awakens and kindles the inspiration or living emotion in men necessary to make them obey the rules of moral conduct, by keeping up, exciting and arousing, the feeling and emotion of unbounded admiration, love, and enthusiasm for the person and character of the first Teacher and Founder of religion which the immediate disciples originally felt. Men rightly call not only the belief in God, but the belief in religion a *faith*, a trust; but a trust in whom? In

the first teacher and founder of their religion who, in Mohammedanism is called the Prophet and in Christianity the Mediator.
If you ask a conscientious Mohammedan why he believes in God and
obeys the rules of moral conduct, he will rightly answer you that he
does it because he believes in Mohammed the Prophet. If you ask a
conscientious Christian why he believes in God and obeys the rules of
moral conduct, he will rightly answer you that he does it because he
loves Christ. Thus you see the belief in Mohammed, the love of
Christ, in fact the feeling and emotion, as I said of unbounded admiration, love, and enthusiasm for the first Teacher and Founder of religion which it is the function of the Church to keep up, excite and
arouse in men—is the source of inspiration, the real power in all the
great religions of the world by which they are able to make men, to
make the mass of mankind obey the rules of moral conduct. *

I have been a long way, but now I can answer the question
which you asked me awhile ago. You asked me, you will remember,
how without a belief in God which religion teaches—how can one
make men, make the mass of mankind, follow and obey the moral rule
which Confucius teaches in his State religion—the absolute duty of
loyalty to the Emperor? I have shown you that it is not the belief in
God taught by religion which really makes men obey moral rules or
rules of moral conduct. I showed you that religion is able to make
men obey the rules of moral conduct principally by means of an organisation called the Church which awakens and kindles in men an
inspiration or living emotion necessary to make them to obey those
rules. Now, in answer to your question I am going to tell you that the
system of the teachings of Confucius, called Confucianism, the State

---

* Mencius, speaking of the two purest and most Christlike characters in Chinese
history, said: "When men heard of the spirit and temper of Po-yi and Shu-ch'i, the dissolute
ruffian became unselfish and the cowardly man had courage." Mencius Bk. III, Part II, IX,
11.

religion in China, like the Church religion in other countries, makes
men obey the rules of moral conduct also by means of an organisation
corresponding to the Church of the Church religion in other
countries. This organisation in the State religion of Confucianism in
China is—the *school*. The school is the Church of the State religion
of Confucius in China. As you know, the same word "*chiao*" in Chinese
for religion is also the word for education. In fact, as the Church
in China is the school, religion to the Chinese means education, culture.
The aim and object of the school in China is not, as in modern
Europe and America to-day, to teach men how to earn a living, how to
make money, but, like the aim and object of the Church religion, to
teach men to understand what Mr. Froude calls the primitive commandment,
"Thou shalt not lie" and "Thou shall not steal"; in fact, to
teach men to be good. "Whether we provide for action or conversation,"
says Dr. Johnson. "whether we wish to be useful or pleasing,
the first requisite is the religious and moral knowledge of right and
wrong; the next, an acquaintance with the history of mankind and
with those examples which may be said to embody truth and prove by
events the reasonableness of opinions."

But then we have seen that the Church of the Church religion is
able to make men obey the rules of moral conduct by awakening and
kindling in men an inspiration or living emotion, and that it awakens
and kindles this inspiration or living emotion principally by exciting
and arousing the feeling and emotion of unbounded admiration, love,
and enthusiasm for the character and person of the first Teacher and
Founder of religion. Now, here there is a difference between the
school—the Church of the State religion of Confucius in China—and
the Church of the Church religion in other countries. The school—
the Church of the State religion in China—it is true, enables and
makes men obey the rules of moral conduct, also like the Church of
the Church religion, by awakening and kindling in men an inspiration

or living emotion. But the means which the school in China uses to awaken and kindle this inspiration or living emotion in men are different from those of the Church of the Church religion in other countries. The school, the Church of the State religion of Confucius in China, does not awaken and kindle this inspiration or living emotion in men by exciting and arousing the feeling of unbounded admiration, love, and enthusiasm for Confucius. Confucius in his lifetime did indeed inspire in his immediate disciples a feeling and emotion of unbounded admiration, love, and enthusiasm, and, after his death, has inspired the same feeling and emotion in all great men who have studied and understood him. But Confucius even while he lived did not inspire, and, after his death, has not inspired in the mass of mankind the same feeling and emotion of admiration, love, and enthusiasm which the founders of all the great religions in the world, as we know, have inspired. The mass of the population in China do not adore and worship Confucius as the mass of the population in Mohammedan countries adore and worship Mohammed, or as the mass of the population in European countries adore and worship Jesus Christ. In this respect Confucius does not belong to the class of men called founders of a religion. In order to be a founder of a religion in the European sense of the word, a man must have an exceptionally or even an abnormally strong emotional nature. Confucius indeed was descended from a race of kings, the house of Shang, the dynasty which ruled over China before the dynasty under which Confucius lived—a race of men who had the strong emotional nature of the Hebrew people. But Confucius himself lived under the dynasty of the House of Chow—a race of men who had the fine intellectual nature of the Greeks, a race of whom the Duke of Chou, the founder, as I told you, of the pre-Confucian religion or religion of the old dispensation in China was a true representative. Thus Confucius was, if I may use a comparison, a Hebrew by birth, with the strong emotional nature of the Hebrew race, who was trained in the best intellectual culture, who had all that which the best intellectual culture of the civilisation of the Greeks could give him. In fact, like the great Goethe in modern Europe, the great Goethe whom the people of Europe will one day recognise as the most perfect type of humanity, the *real European* which the civilisation of Europe has produced, as the Chinese have acknowledged Confucius to be the most perfect type of humanity, the *real Chinaman*, which the Chinese civilisation has produced—like the great Goethe, I say, Confucius was too educated and cultured a man to belong to the class of men called founders of religion. Indeed, even while he lived Confucius was not known to be what he was, except by his most intimate and immediate disciples.

The school in China, I say, the Church of the State religion of Confucius, does not awaken and kindle the inspiration or living emotion necessary to make men obey the rules of moral conduct by exciting and arousing the feeling and emotion of admiration, love, and enthusiasm for Confucius. But then how does the school in China awaken and kindle the inspiration or living emotion necessary to make man obey the rules of moral conduct? Confucius says: "In education the feeling and emotion is aroused by the study of *poetry*; the judgement is formed by the study of good taste and good manners; the education of the character is completed by the study of music." The school— the Church of the State religion in China—awakens and kindles the inspiration or living emotion in men necessary to make them obey the rules of moral conduct by teaching them poetry—in fact, the works of all really great men in literature, which, as I told you, has the inspiration or living emotion that is in the rules of moral conduct of religion. Matthew Arnold, speaking of Homer and the quality of *nobleness* in his poetry, says: "The nobleness in the poetry of Homer and of the few great men in literature can refine the raw, natural man, can *transmute* him." In fact, whatsoever things are true, whatsoever things are just, whatsoever things are pure, whatsoever things are lovely, whatsoever things are of good report, if there be any virtue and if there be any praise—the school, the Church of the State religion in China, makes men think on these things, and in making them think on these things, awakens and kindles the inspiration or living emotion necessary to enable and make them obey the rules of moral conduct.

But then you will remember I told you that the works of really great men in literature, such as the poetry of Homer, cannot reach the mass of mankind, because all great men in literature speak the language of educated men which the mass of mankind cannot understand. Such being the case, how then does the system of the teachings of Confucius, Confucianism, the State Religion in China, awaken and kindle in the mass of mankind, in the mass of the population in China, the inspiration or living emotion necessary to enable and make them obey the rules of moral conduct? Now, I told you that the organisation in the State Religion of Confucius in China corresponding to the Church of the Church Religion in other countries, is the School. But that is not quite correct. The real organisation in the State Religion of Confucius in China corresponding exactly to the Church of the Church Religion in other countries is—the *Family*. The real Church—of which the School is but an adjunct—the real and true Church of the State Religion of Confucius in China, is the Family with its ancestral tablet or chapel in every house, and its ancestral Hall or Temple in every village and town. I have shown you that the source of inspiration, the real motive power by which all the great Religions of the world are able to make men, to make the mass of mankind obey the rules of moral conduct, is the feeling and emotion of unbounded admiration, love and enthusiasm which it is the function of the Church to excite and arouse in men for the first Teachers and Founders of those Religions. Now the source of inspiration, the real motive power by which the State Religion of Confucius in China is able to make men, to enable and make the mass of the population in China obey the rules of moral conduct is the "Love for their father and mother." The Church of the Church Religion, Christianity, says: "Love Christ." The Church of the State Religion of Confucius in China—the ancestral tablet in every family—says "Love your father and your mother." St. Paul says:—"Let every man that names the name of Christ depart from iniquity." But the author of the book on Filial Piety(孝经), written in the Han dynasty, the counterpart of the *Imitatio Christi* in China, says: "Let everyone who loves his father and mother depart from iniquity." In short, as the essence, the motive power, the source of real inspiration of the Church religion, Christianity, is the Love of Christ, so the essence, the motive power, the source of real inspiration of the State Religion, Confucianism in China, is the "Love of father and mother"— Filial Piety, with its cult of ancestor worship.

Confucius says: "To gather in the same place where our fathers before us have gathered; to perform the same ceremonies which they before us have performed; to play the same music which they before us have played; to pay respect to those whom they honoured; to love those who were dear to them; in fact, to serve them now dead as if they were living, and now departed, as if they were still with us, that is the highest achievement of Filial Piety." Confucius, further says:—"By cultivating respect for the dead, and carrying the memory back to the distant past, the good in the people will grow deep." *Cogitavi dies antiquos, et annos eternos in menti habui.* That is how the State Religion in China, Confucianism, awakens and kindles in men, the inspiration or living emotion necessary to enable and make them obey the rules of moral conduct, the highest and most important of all these rules being the absolute Duty of Loyalty to the Emperor, just as the highest and most important rules of moral conduct in all the Great Religions of the world is fear of God. In other words, the Church Religion, Christianity, says:—"Fear God and obey Him." But the State Religion of Confucius, or Confucianism, says:—"Honour the Emperor and be loyal to him." The Church Religion, Christianity, says:—"If you want to fear God and obey Him, you must first love Christ." The State Religion of Confucius, or Confucianism, say:—"If you want to honour the Emperor and be loyal to him, you must first love your father and mother."

Now I have shown you why it is that there is no conflict between the heart and the head in the Chinese civilisation for these last 2,500 years since Confucius' time. The reason why there is no such conflict is because the Chinese people, even the mass of the population in China, do not feel the need of Religion—I mean Religion in the European sense of the word; and the reason why the Chinese people do not feel the need of religion is because the Chinese people have in Confucianism something which can take the place of Religion. That something, I have shown you, is the principle of absolute Duty of Loyalty to the Emperor; the Code of Honour called *Ming fen ta yi*, which Confucius teaches in the State Religion which he has given to the Chinese nation. The greatest service, I said, which Confucius has done for the Chinese people is in giving them this State Religion in which he taught the absolute Duty of Loyalty to the Emperor.

Thus much I have thought it necessary to say about Confucius and what he has done for the Chinese nation, because it has a very important bearing upon the subject of our present discussion, the Spirit of the Chinese People. For I want to tell you and you will understand it from what I have told you, that a Chinaman, especially if he is an educated man, who knowingly forgets, gives up or throws away the Code of Honour, the *Ming fen ta yi* in the State Religion of Confucius in China, Which teaches the absolute Divine Duty of Loyalty to the Emperor or Sovereign to whom he has once given his allegiance, such a Chinaman is a man who has lost the spirit of the Chinese people, the spirit of his nation and race: *he is no longer a real Chinaman*.

Finally, let me shortly sum up what I want to say on the subject of our present discussion—the Spirit of the Chinese People or what is the real Chinaman. The real Chinaman, I have shown you, is a man who lives the life of a man of adult reason with the simple heart of a child, and the Spirit of the Chinese people is a happy union of soul with intellect. Now if you will examine the products of the Chinese mind in their standard works of art and literature, you will find that it is this happy union of soul with the intellect which makes them so satisfying and delightful. What Matthew Arnold says of the poetry of Homer is true of all Chinese standard literature, that "it has not only the power of profoundly touching that natural heart of humanity, which it is the weakness of Voltaire that he cannot reach, but can also address the understanding with all Voltaire's admirable simplicity and rationality."

Matthew Arnold calls the poetry of the best Greek poets the priestess of imaginative reason. Now the spirit of the Chinese people, as it is seen in the best specimens of the products of their art and literature, is really what Matthew Arnold calls imaginative reason. Matthew Arnold says:—"The poetry of later Paganism lived by the senses and understanding: the poetry of medieval Christianity lived by the heart and imagination. But the main element of the modern spirit's life, of the modern European spirit to-day, is neither the senses and understanding, nor the heart and imagination, it is the imaginative reason."

Now if it is true what Matthew Arnold says here that the element by which the modern spirit of the people of Europe to-day, if it would live right—has to live, is imaginative reason, then you can see how valuable for the people of Europe this Spirit of the Chinese people is,—this spirit which Matthew Arnold calls imaginative reason. How valuable it is, I say, and how important it is that you should study it, try to understand it, love it, instead of ignoring, despising and trying to destroy it.

But now before I finally conclude, I want to give you a warning. I want to warn you that when you think of this Spirit of the Chinese People, which I have tried to explain to you, you should bear in mind that it is not a science, philosophy, theosophy, or any "ism," like the theosophy or "ism" of Madame Blavatsky or Mrs. Besant. The Spirit of the Chinese People is not even what you would call a mentality— an active working of the brain and mind. The Spirit of the Chinese People, I want to tell you, is a state of mind, a temper of the soul, which you cannot learn as you learn shorthand or Esperanto—in short, a mood, or in the words of the poet, a serene and blessed mood.

Now last of all I want to ask your permission to recite to you a few lines of poetry from the most Chinese of the English poets, Wordsworth, which better than anything I have said or can say, will describe to you the serene and blessed mood which is the Spirit of the Chinese People. These few lines of the English poet will put before you in a way I cannot hope to do, that happy union of soul with in- tellect in the Chinese type of humanity, that serene and blessed mood which gives to the real Chinaman his inexpressible gentleness. Wordsworth in his lines on Tintern Abbey says:—

"...nor less, I trust

To them I may have owed another gift
Of aspect more sublime: that blessed mood
In which the burthen of the mystery,
In which the heavy and the weary weight
Of all this unintelligible world,
Is lightened:—that serene and blessed mood
In which the affections gently lead us on,—

64

Until, the breath of this corporeal frame
And even motion of our human blood
Almost suspended, we are laid asleep
In body, and become a living soul:
While with an eye made quiet by the power
Of harmony, and the deep power of joy,
We see into the life of things."

The serene and blessed mood which enables us *to see into the life of things*: that is imaginative reason, that is the Spirit of the Chinese People.

THE CHINESE WOMAN

Matthew Arnold, speaking of the argument taken from the Bible which was used in the House of Commons to support the Bill for enabling a man to marry his deceased wife's sister, said: "Who will believe when he really considers the matter, that when the feminine nature, the feminine ideal and our relations with them are brought into question, the delicate and apprehensive genius of the Indo-European race, the race which invented the Muses, and Chivalry, and the Madonna, is to find its last word on this question in the institution of a Semitic people whose wisest King had seven hundred wives and three hundred concubines?"

The two words I want for my purpose here from the above long quotation are the words "feminine ideal." Now what is the Chinese feminine ideal? What is the Chinese people's ideal of the feminine nature and their relations to that ideal? But before going further, let me, with all deference to Matthew Arnold, and respect for his Indo-European race, say here that the feminine ideal of the Semitic race, of the old Hebrew people is not such a horrid one as Matthew Arnold would have us infer from the fact that their wisest King had a multitude of wives and concubines. For here is the feminine ideal of the old Hebrew people, as we find it in their literature: "Who can find a virtuous woman? for her price is far above rubies. The heart of her husband doth safely trust in her. She rises also while it is yet night and giveth meat to her household and a portion to her maidens. She layeth her hands to the spindle and her fingers hold the distaff. She is not afraid of snow for her household ; for *all her household are clothed in scarlet*. She openeth her mouth with wisdom and *in her tongue is the law of kindness.* She looketh well to the ways of her household and eateth not the bread of idleness. Her children rise up and call her blessed, her husband also and he praiseth her."

This, I think, is not such a horrid, not such a bad ideal after all, — this feminine ideal of the Semitic race. It is of course not so etherial as the Madonna and the Muses, the feminine ideal of the Indo-European race. However, one must, I think, admit, — the Madonna and the Muses are very well to hang up as pictures in one's room, but if you put a broom into the hands of the Muses or send your Madonna into the kitchen, you will be sure to have your rooms in a mess and you will probably get in the morning no breakfast at all. Confucius says, "The ideal is not away from the actuality of human life. When men take something away from the actuality of human life as the ideal, — that is not the true ideal." * But if the Hebrew feminine ideal cannot be compared with the Madonna and the Muses, it can very well, I think, compare with the modern European feminine ideal, the feminine ideal of the Indo-European race in Europe and America to-day. I will not speak of the suffragettes in England. But compare the old Hebrew feminine ideal with the modern feminine ideal such as one finds it in modern novels, with the heroine, for instance of Dumas' *Dame aux Camelias.* By the way, it may interest people to know that of all the books in European literature which have been translated into Chinese, the novel of Dumas with the Madonna of the Mud as the superlative feminine ideal has had the greatest sale and success in the present up-to-date modern China. This French novel called in Chinese the *Cha-hua-nu* (茶花女) has even been dramatised and put on the stage in all the up-to-date Chinese theatres in China. Now if you will compare the old feminine ideal of the Semitic race, the woman who is not afraid of the

* 中庸 The Universal Order XIII.

snow for her household, for she has clothed them all in scarlet, with the feminine ideal of the Indo-European race in Europe to-day, the Camelia Lady who has no household, and therefore clotheth not her household, but herself in scarlet and goes with a Camelia flower on her breast to be photographed: then you will understand what is true and what is false, tinsel civilisation.

Nay, even if you will compare the old Hebrew feminine ideal, the woman who layeth her hands to the spindle and whose fingers hold the distaff, who looketh well to the ways of her household and eateth not the bread of idleness, with the up-to-date modern Chinese woman who layeth her hands on the piano and whose fingers hold a big bouquet, who, dressed in tight fitting yellow dress with a band of tinsel gold around her head, goes to show herself and sing before a miscellaneous crowd in the Confucian Association Hall: if you compare these two feminine ideals, you will then know how fast and far modern China is drifting away from true civilisation. For the womanhood in a nation is the flower of the civilisation, of the state of civilisation in that nation.

But now to come to our question : what is the Chinese feminine ideal? The Chinese feminine ideal I answer, is essentially the same as the old Hebrew feminine ideal with one important difference of which I will speak later on. The Chinese feminine ideal is the same as the old Hebrew ideal in that it is not an ideal merely for hanging up as a picture in one's room; nor an ideal for a man to spend his whole life in caressing and worshipping. The Chinese feminine ideal is an ideal with a broom in her hands to sweep and clean the rooms with. In fact the Chinese written character for a wife (妇) is composed of two radicals — (女) meaning a woman and (帚) meaning a broom. In classical Chinese, in what I have called the official uniform Chinese, a wife is called the Keeper of the Provision Room—a Mistress of the Kitchen (主中馈). Indeed the true feminine ideal,—the feminine ideal of all people with a true, not tinsel civilisation, such as the old Hebrews, the ancient Greeks and the Romans, is essentially the same as the Chinese feminine ideal: the true feminine ideal is always the *Hausfrau*, the house wife, *la dame de menage or chatelaine*.

But now to go more into details. The Chinese feminine ideal, as it is handed down from the earliest times, is summed up in three obediences (三从) and Four Virtues (四德). Now what are the four virtues? They are: first womanly character (女德); second, womanly conversation (女言); third, womanly appearance (女容); and lastly, womanly work (女工). Womanly character means not extraordinary talents or intelligence, but modesty, cheerfulness, chastity, constancy, orderliness, blameless conduct and perfect manners. Womanly conversation means not eloquence or brilliant talk, but refined choice of words, never to use coarse or violent language, to know when to speak and when to stop speaking. Womanly appearance means not beauty or prettiness of face, but personal cleanliness and faultlessness in dress and attire. Lastly, womanly work means not any special skill or ability, but assiduous attention to the spinning room, never to waste time in laughing and giggling and work in the kitchen to prepare clean and wholesome food, especially when there are guests in the house. These are the four essentials in the conduct of a woman as laid down in the "Lessons for Women" (女诫), written by Ts'ao Ta Ku (曹大家) or Lady Ts'ao, sister of the great historian Pan Ku (班固) of the Han Dynasty.

Then again what do the Three Obediences (三从) in the Chinese feminine ideal mean? They mean really three self sacrifices or "live for's?" That is to say, when a woman is unmarried, she is to live for her father (在家从父); when married, she is to live for her husband (出嫁从夫); and, as a widow, she is to live for her children (夫死从子). In fact, the chief end of a woman in China is not to live for herself, or for society; not to be a reformer or to be president of the woman's natural feet Society; not to live even as a saint or to do good to the world; the chief end of a woman in China is to live as a good daughter, a good wife and a good mother.

A foreign lady friend of mine once wrote and asked me whether it is true that we Chinese believe, like the Mohammedans, that a woman has no soul. I wrote back and told her that we Chinese do not hold that a woman has no soul, but that we hold that a woman, —a true Chinese woman has no *self*. Now speaking of this "no self" in the Chinese woman leads me to say a few words on a very difficult subject, —a subject which is not only difficult, but, I am afraid almost impossible for people with the modern European education to understand, viz. concubinage in China. This subject of concubinage, I am afraid, is not only a difficult, but also a dangerous subject to discuss in public. But, as the English poet says.

Thus fools rush in where angels fear to tread,

I will try my best here to explain why concubinage in China is not such an immoral custom as people generally imagine.

The first thing I want to say on this subject of concubinage is that it is the selflessness in the Chinese woman which makes concubinage in China not only possible, but also *no immoral*. But, before I go further, let me tell you here, that concubinage in China does not mean having many *wives*. By Law in China, a man is allowed to have only *one* wife, but he may have as many handmaids or concubines as he like. In Japanese a handmaid or concubine is called *te-kaki*, *a hand rack or me-kaki* an eye rack;—i.e. to say, a rack where to rest your hands or eyes on when you are tired. Now the feminine ideal in China, I said, is not an ideal for a man to spend his whole life in caressing and worshipping. The Chinese feminine ideal is, for a wife to live absolutely, selflessly for her husband. Therefore when a husband who is sick or invalided from overwork with his brain and mind, requires a handmaid, a hand rack or eye rack to enable him to get well and to fit him for his life work, the wife in China with her selflessness, gives it to him just as a good wife in Europe and America gives an armchair or goat's milk to her husband when he is sick or requires it. In fact it is the selflessness of the wife in China, her sense of duty, the duty of self sacrifice which allows a man in China to have handmaids or concubines.

But people will say to me, "why ask selflessness and sacrifice only from the woman? What about the man?" To this. I answer, does not the man, — the husband, who toils and moils to support his family, and especially if he is a gentleman, who has to do his duty not only to his family, but to his King and country, and, in doing that has, some time even to give his life: does he not also make sacrifice? The Emperor Kanghsi in a valedictory decree which he issued on his death bed, said that "he did not know until then what a life of sacrifice the life of an Emperor in China is." And yet, let me say here by the way, Messrs. J. B. Bland and Backhouse in their latest book have described this Emperor Kanghsi as a huge, helpless, horrid Brigham Young, who was dragged into his grave by the multitude of his wives and children. But, of course, for modern men like Messrs. J. P. Bland and Backhouse, concubinage is inconceivable except as something horrid, vile and nasty, because the diseased imagination of such men can conceive of nothing except nasty, vile and horrid things. But that is neither here nor there. Now what I want to say here is that the life of every *true* man—from the Emperor down to the ricksha coolie—and every *true* woman, is a life of sacrifice. The sacrifice of a woman in China is to live selflessly for the man whom she calls husband, and the sacrifice of the man in China is to provide for, to protect at all costs the woman or women whom he has taken into his house and also the children they may bear him. Indeed to people who talk of the immorality of concubinage in China, I would say that to me the Chinese mandarin who keeps concubines is less selfish, less immoral than the European in his motor car, who picks up a helpless woman from the public street and, after amusing himself with her for one night, throws her away again on the pavement of the public street the next morning. The Chinese mandarin with his concubines may be selfish, but he at least provides a house for his concubines and holds himself for life responsible for the maintenance of the women he keeps. In fact, if the mandarin is selfish, I say that the European in his motor car is not only selfish, but a *coward*. Ruskin says, "The honour of a true soldier is verily not to be able to slay, but to be willing and ready at all times to *be slain*. "In the same way I say, the honour of a woman—a true woman in China, is not only to love and be true to her husband, but to live absolutely, selflessly for him. In fact, this Religion of Selflessness is the religion of the woman, especially, the gentlewoman or lady in China, as the Religion of Loyalty which I have tried elsewhere to explain, is the religion of the man,—the gentleman in China. Until foreigners come to understand these two religions, the "Religion of Loyalty and the Religion of Selflessness" of the Chinese people, they can never understand the real Chinaman, or the real Chinese woman.

But people will again say to me, "What about love? Can a man who really loves his wife have the heart to have other women besides her in his house?" To this I answer, yes, — Why not? For the real test that a husband really loves his wife is not that he should spend his whole life in lying down at her feet and caressing her. The real test whether a man truly loves his wife is whether he is anxious and tries in every thing reasonable, not only to protect her, but also not to hurt her, not to hurt her feelings. Now to bring a strange woman into the house must hurt the wife, hurt her feelings. But here, I say, it is what I have called the Religion of selflessness which protects the wife from being hurt: it is this absolute selflessness in the woman in China which makes it possible for her not to feel hurt when she sees her husband bring another woman into the house. In other words, it is the selflessness in the wife in China which enables, *permits* the husband to take a concubine without hurting the wife. For here, let me point out, a gentleman, —a real gentleman in China, never takes a concubine without the consent of his wife and a real gentlewoman or lady in China whenever there is a proper reason that her husband should take a concubine, will never refuse to give her consent. I know of many cases where having no children the husband after middle age wanted to take a concubine, but because the wife refused to give her consent, desisted. I know even of a case where the husband, because he did not want to exact this mark of selflessness from his wife who was sick and in bad health, refused, when urged by the wife, to take a concubine, but the wife, without his knowledge and consent, not only bought a concubine, but actually forced him to take the concubine into the house. In fact, the protection for the wife against the abuse of concubinage in China is the *love of her husband for her*. Instead, therefore of saying that husbands in China cannot truly love their wives because they take concubines, one should rather say it is because the husband in China so *truly* loves his wife that he has the privilege and liberty of taking concubines without fear of his abusing that privilege and liberty. This liberty, this privilege is sometimes and even—when the sense of honour in the men in the nation is low as now in this anarchic China, often abused. But still I say the protection for the wife in China where the husband is allowed to take a concubine, is the love of her husbaud for her, the love of her husband, and, I must add here, his *tact* —the perfect good taste in the real Chinese gentleman. I wonder if one man in a thousand among the ordinary Europeans and Americans, who can keep more than one woman in the same house without turning the house into a fighting cockpit or hell. In short, it is this tact, —the perfect good taste in the real Chinese gentleman which makes it possible for the wife in China not to feel hurt, when the husband takes and keeps a handmaid, a hand rack, an eye rack in the same house with her. But to sum up, —it is the Religion of selflessness, the absolute selflessness of the woman, —the gentlewoman or lady and the love of the husband for his wife and his tact, —the perfect good taste of a real Chinese gentleman, which, as I said, makes concubinage in China, not only possible, but also *not immoral*. Confucius said, "The Law of the Gentleman takes its rise from the relation between the husband and the wife."

Now in order to convince those who might still be sceptical that husbands in China *truly* love, can *deeply* love their wives, I could produce abundant proofs from Chinese history and literature. For this purpose I should particularly like to quote and translate here an elegy written on the death of his wife by Yuan Chen (元稹), a poet of the T'ang dynasty. But unfortunately the piece is too long for quotation here in this already too long article. Those acquainted with Chinese, however, who wish to know how deep the affection, —affection, true love and not sexual passion which in modern times is often mistaken for love, —how deep the love of a husband in China for his wife is, should read this elegy which can be found in any ordinary collection of the T'ang poets. The title of the elegy is, (遣悲怀)— "Lines to ease the aching heart." But as I cannot use this elegy for my purpose, I will, instead, give here a short poem of four lines written by a modern poet who was once a secretary of the late Viceroy Chang Chih-tung. The poet went togther with his wife in the suite of the Viceroy to Wuchang and after staying there many years, his wife died. Immediately after he too had to leave Wuchang. He wrote the poem on leaving Wuchang. The words in Chinese are

此恨人人有

百年能有几

痛哉长江水
同渡不同归

The meaning in English is something like this:—

> This grief is common to everyone,
> One hundred years how many can attain?
> But 'tis heart breaking, o waters of the Yangtze,
> Together we came,—but together we return not.

The feeling here is as deep, if not deeper; but the words are fewer, and the language is simpler, even than Tennyson's.

> Break, break, break
> On the cold grey stones, O sea!
> ……
> But O for the touch of a vanished hand,
> And the sound of a voice that is still!

But now what about the love of a wife in China for her husband? I do not think any evidence is needed to prove this. It is true that in China the bride and bride-groom as a rule never see each other until the marriage day, and yet that there is love between even bride and bride-groom, can be seen in these four lines of poetry from the T'ang dynasty:—

洞房昨夜停红烛
待晓堂前拜舅姑
妆罢低声问夫婿
画眉深浅入时无

The meaning in English of the above is something like this,

> In the bridal chamber last night stood red candles;
> Waiting for the morning to salute the father and
>   mother in the hall,
> Toilet finished,—in a low voice she asks her sweet-

> heart husband,
>
> "*Are the shades in my painted eyebrows quite à la mode?*"

But here in order to understand the above, I must tell you something about marriage in China. There are in every legal marriage in China six ceremonies (六礼): first, (问名) asking for the name, i. e., formal proposal; second (纳彩) receiving the silk presents, i. e., betrothal: third (定期) fixing the day of marriage; fourth (亲迎) fetching the bride; fifth (奠雁) pouring libation before the wild goose, i. e., plighting troth, so-called because the wild goose is supposed to be most faithful in connubial love; sixth (庙见)— temple presentation. Of these six ceremonies, the last two are the most important, I shall therefore here describe them more in detail.

The fourth ceremony, fetching the bride at the present day, is, except in my province Fukien where we keep up the old customs, — generally dispensed with, as it entails too much trouble and expense to the bride's family. The bride now, instead of being fetched, is sent to the bride-groom's house. When the bride arrives there, the bride-groom receives her at the gate and himself opens the door of the bridal chair and leads her to the hall of the house. There the bride and bride-groom worship Heaven and Earth (拜天地), i. e. to say, they fall on their kness with their faces turned to the door of the hall with a table carrying two red burning candles before the open sky and then the hushand pours libations on the ground, —in presence of the pair of wild geese (if wild goose cannot be had, an ordinary goose) which the bride has brought with her. This is the ceremony called *Tien yen* pouring libation before the wild goose; plighting of troth between man and woman—he vowing to be true to her, and she, to be true to him, just as faithful as the pair of wild geese they see before them. From this moment, they become, so to speak, natural *sweetheart husband*

and *sweetheart wife*, bound only by the moral law, the Law of the Gentleman, — the word of honour which they have given to each other, but not yet by the *Civic* Law. This ceremony therefore may be called the moral or Religious marriage.

After this comes the ceremony called the (交拜) mutual salutation between bride and bride-groom. The bride standing on the right side of the hall first goes on her knees before the bride-groom, — he going on his knees to her at the same time. Then they change places. The bride-groom now standing where the bride stood, *goes on his knees to her*, — she returning the salute just as he did. Now this ceremony of *chiao pai* mutual salutation, I wish to point out here, proves beyond all doubt that in China there is *perfect equality* between man and woman, between husband and wife.

As I said before, the ceremony of plighting troth may be called the moral or Religious marriage as distinguished from what may called the *civic* marriage, which comes three days after. — In the moral or religious marriage, the man and woman becomes husband and wife before the moral Law—before God. The contract so far is solely between the man and woman. The State or, as in China, the Family takes the place of the State in all social and civic life—the State acting only as Court of appeal, — the Family takes no cognisance of the marriage or contract between the man and woman here in this, what I have called the moral or religious marriage. In fact on this first day and until the *civic* marriage takes place on the third day of the marriage, the bride is not only *not* introduced, but also not allowed to see or be seen by the members of the bride-groom's family.

Thus for two days and two nights the bride-groom and the bride in China live, so to speak not as legal, but, as *sweetheart-husband* and *sweetheart-wife*. On the third day, — then comes the last ceremony in the Chinese marriage—the *Miao-chien*, the temple presentation or civic marriage. I say, on the third day because that is the rule de *riguer* as laid down in the Book of Rites (三日庙见). But now to save trouble and expense, it is generally performed on the day after. This ceremony—the temple presentation, takes place, when the ancestral temple of the family clan is nearby,—of course in the ancestral temple. But for people living in towns and cities where there is no ancestral temple of the family clan nearby, the ceremony is performed before the miniature ancestral chapel or shrine—which is in the house of every respectable family, even the poorest in China. This ancestral temple, chapel or shrine with a tablet or red piece of paper on the wall, as I have said elsewhere, is the *church* of the State Religion of Confucius in China corresponding to the church of the Church Religion in Christian countries.

This ceremony—the temple presentation begins by the father of the bridegroom or failing him, the nearest senior member of the family, going on his knees before the ancestral tablet—thus announcing to the spirits of the dead ancestors that a young member of the family has now brought a wife home into the family. Then the bridegroom and bride one after the other, each goes on his and her knees before the same ancestral tablet. From this moment the man and woman becomes husband and wife,—not only before the moral Law or God,—but before the Family, before the State, before Civic Law. I have therefore called this ceremony of *miao chien*, temple presentation in the Chinese marriage,—the civic or civil marriage. Before this civic or civil marriage, the woman, the bride,—according to the Book of Rites,—is not a legal wife (不庙见不成妇). When the bride happens to die before this ceremony of temple presentation, she is not allowed—according to the Book of Rites—to be buried in the family burying ground of her husband and her memorial tablet is not put up in the ancestral temple of his family clan.

Thus we see the contract in a legal civic marriage in China is not between the woman and the man. The contract is between the woman and the family of her husband. She is not married to him, but *into his family*. In the visiting card of a Chinese lady in China, she does not write, for instance, Mrs. Ku Hung-ming, but literally "Miss Feng, gone to the home of the family (originally from) Tsin An adjusts her dress." (归晋安冯氏裣衽)—The contract of marriage in China being *between the woman and the family of her husband*,—the husband and wife can neither of them repudiate the contract without the consent of the husband's family. This I want to point out here, is the fundamental difference between a marriage in China and a marriage in Europe and America. The marriage in Europe and America,—is what we Chinese would call a sweet-heart marriage, a marriage, bound solely by love between the individual man and the individual woman. But in China the marriage is, as I have said, a civic marriage, a contract not between the woman and the man, *but between the woman and the family of her husband*, —in which she has obligations not only to him, but also to his family, and through the family, to society, —to the social or civic order; in fact, to the State. Finally let me point out here that it is this civic conception of marriage which gives solidarity and stability to the family, to the social or civic order, to the State in China. Until therefore, let me be permitted to say here, — the people in Europe and America understand what true *civic life* means, understand and have a true conception of what it is really to be a citizen, — a citizen not each one living for himself, but each one living first for his family, and through that for the civic order or State, —there can then be no such thing as a stable society, civic order or State in the true sense of the word. —A State such as we see it in modern Europe and American to-day, where the men and woman have not a true conception of civic life, —such a State with all its parliament and machinery of government, may be called, if you like, —a big Commercial Concern, or as it really is, in times of war, a gang of brigands and pirates, —but not a State. In fact, I may be permitted further to say here, it is the false conception of a State as a big commercial concern having only the selfish material interests of those who have the biggest shares in the concern to be considered, —this false conception of a State with the *esprit de corps* of brigands, which is, at bottom, the cause of the terrible war now going on in Europe. In short, without a true conception of civic life there can be no true State and without a true State, how can there be civilisation. To us Chinese, a man who does not marry, who has no family, no home which he has to defend, cannot be a patriot, and if calls himself a patriot, —we Chinese call him a *brigand patriot*. In fact in order to have a true conception of a State or civic order, one must first have a true conception of a family, and to have a true conception of a family, of family life, one must first of all have a true conception of marriage, —marriage not as a sweetheart marriage, but as a civic marrage which I have in the above tried to describe.

But to return from the digression. Now you can picture to yourself how the sweet-heart wife waiting for the morning—to salute the father and mother of her husband, toilet finished, in a low voice, whispers to her sweet-heart husband and asks if her eyebrows are painted quite à la mode—Here you see, I say, there is love between husband and wife in China, although they have not seen each other before the marriage—even on the third day of the marriage. But if you think the love in the above is not deep enough, then take just these two lines of poetry from a wife to her absent husband.

当君怀归日
是妾断肠时

The day when you think of coming home.
Ah! then my heart will already be broken.

Roselind in Shakespeare's "As You Like It" says to her cousin Celia: "O coz, coz, my pretty little coz, that thou knowest how many fathom deep I am in love! But I cannot be sounded: my affection hath an unknown bottom, like the bay of Portugal." Now the love of a woman, —of a wife for her husband in China and also the love of the man—of the husband for his wife in China, one can truly say, is like Rosolind's love, many fathom deep and cannot be sounded; it has an unknown bottom like the bay of Portugal.

But, I will now speak of the difference which, I said, there is between the Chinese feminine ideal and the feminine ideal of the old Hebrew people. The Hebrew lover in the Songs of Solomon, thus addresses his lady-love: "Thou art beautiful, O my love, as Tirzah, comely as Jerusalem, *terrible as an army with banners*!" People who have seen beautiful dark-eyed Jewesses even to day, will acknowledge the truth and graphicness of the picture which the old Hebrew lover here gives of the feminine ideal of his race. But in and about the Chinese feminine ideal, I want to say here, there is nothing *terrible* either in a physical or in a moral sense. Even the Helen of Chinese history, —the beauty, who with one glance brings down a city and with another glance destroys a kingdom (一顾倾人城再顾倾人国) she is terrible only mataphorically. In an essay on "the Spirit of the Chinese People," I said that the one word which will sum up the total impression which the Chinese type of humanity makes upon you is the English word, "gentle." If this is true of the real Chinaman, it is truer of the real Chinese woman. In fact this "gentleness" of the real Chinaman, in the Chinese woman, becomes sweet *meekness*. The meekness, the submissiveness of the woman in China is like that of Milton's Eve in the "Paradise Lost," who says to her husband,

> *God is thy law, thou, mine; to know no more*
> *Is woman's happiest knowledge and her praise.*

Indeed this quality of perfect meekness in the Chinese feminine ideal you will find in the feminine ideal of no other people, —of no other civilisation, Hebrew, Greek or Roman. This perfect, *divine* meekness in the Chinese feminine ideal you will find only in one civilisation, —the Christian civilisation, when that civilisation in Europe reached its perfection, during the period of the *Renaissance*. If you will read the beautiful story of Griselda in Boccacio's *Decameron* and see the true Christian feminine ideal shown there, you will then understand what this perfect submissiveness, this *divine* meekness, meekness to the point of absolute selflessness, —in the Chinese feminine ideal means. In short, in this quality of divine meekness, the *true* Christian feminine ideal is the Chinese feminine ideal, with just a shade of difference. If you will carefully compare the picture of the Christian Madonna with, —not the Budhist Kuan Yin, —but with the pictures of women fairies and genii painted by famous Chinese artists, you will be able to see this difference, —the difference between the Christian feminine ideal, and the Chinese feminine ideal. The Christian Madonna is meek and so is the Chinese feminine ideal. The Christian Madonna is etherial and so is the Chinese feminine ideal. But the Chinese feminine ideal is more than all that; the Chinese feminine ideal is *debonair*. To have a conception of what this charm and grace expressed by the word debonair mean, you will have to go to ancient Greece,

— *o ubi campi Spercheosque et virginibus bacchata Lacaenis Taygeta*!

In fact you will have to go to the fields of Thessaly and the streams of Spercheios, to the hills alive with the dances of the Laconian maidens, —the hills of Taygetus.

Indeed I want to say here that even now in China since the period of the Sung Dynasty (A. D. 960), when what may be called the Confucian Puritanism of the Sung philosphers has narrowed, petrified, and in a way, *vulgarised* the spirit of Confucianism, the spirit of the Chinese civilisation—since then, the womanhood in China has lost much of the grace and charm, —expressed by the word *debonair*. Therefore *if you want to see the grace and charm expressed by the word debonair in the true Chinese feminine ideal, you will have to go to Japan where the women there at least, even to this* day, have preserved the pure Chinese civilisation of the T'ang Dynasty. It is this grace and charm expressed by the word debonair combined with the *divine meekness* of the Chinese feminine ideal, which gives the air of *distinction* (名贵) to the *Japanese* woman, — even to the poorest Japanese woman to-day.

In connection with this quality of charm and grace expressed by the word debonair, allow me to quote to you here a few words from Matthew Arnold with which he contrasts the *brick-and-mortar* Protestant English feminine ideal with the delicate Catholic French feminine ideal. Comparing Eugénie de Guerin, the beloved sister of the French poet Maurice de Guerin, with an English woman who wrote poetry, Miss Emma Tatham, —Matthew Arnold says: " The French woman is a Catholic in Languedoc; the English woman is a Protestant at Margate, Margate the brick and mortar image of English Protestantism, representing it in all its prose, all its uncomeliness, —and let me add, all its salubrity. Between the external form and fashion of these two lives, between the Catholic Madlle de Guerin's *nadalet* at the Languedoc Christmas, her chapel of moss at Easter time, her daily reading of the life of a saint, —between all this and the bare, blank, narrowly English setting of Miss Tatham's Protestantism, her "union in Church fellowship with the worshippers at Hawley Square, Margate," her singing with the soft, sweet voice, the animating lines:

> *My Jesus to know, and feel His Blood flow*
> *' Tis life everlasting, ' tis heaven below!* "

her young female teachers belonging to the Sunday school and her

"Mr. Thomas Rowe, a venerable class-leader" —what a dissimilarity. In the ground of the two lives, a likeness; in all their circumstances, what unlikeness! An unlikeness, it will be said, in that which is non-essential and indifferent. Non-essential, — yes; indifferent, —no. The signal *want of grace and charm* — in the English Protestantism's setting of its religious life is not an indifferent matter; it is a real weakness. *This ought ye to have done, and not to have left the other undone.*"

Last of all I wish to point out to you here the most important quality of all, in the Chinese feminine ideal, the quality which preeminently distinguishes her from the feminine ideal of all other people or nations ancient or modern. This quality in the women in China, it is true, is common to the feminine ideal of every people or nation with any pretension to civilisation, but this quality, I want to say here, developed in the Chinese feminine ideal to such a degree of perfection as you will find it nowhere else in the world. This quality of which I speak, is described by the two Chinese words *yu hsien*（幽閑）which, in the quotation I gave above from the "Lessons for Women," by Lady T'sao, —I translated as modesty and cheerfulness. The Chinese word *yu*（幽）literally means retired, secluded, occult and the word *hsien*（閑）literally means "at ease or leisure." For the Chinese word *yu*, —the English "modesty, bashfulness" only gives you an idea of its meaning. The German word *Sittsamkeit* comes nearer to it. But perhaps the French *pudeur* comes nearest to it of all. This *pudeur*, I may say here, this bashfulness, the quality expressed by the Chinese word *yu*（幽）is the essence of all womanly qualities. The more a woman has this quality of *pudeur* developed in her, the more she has of womanliness, —of femininity, in fact, the more she is a perfect or ideal woman. When on the contrary a woman loses this quality expressed by the Chinese word *yu*（幽）, loses this bashfulness, this *pudeur*, she then loses altogether her womanliness, her femininity, and with that, her perfume, her fragrance and becomes a mere piece of human meat or flesh. Thus, it is this *pudeur*, this quality expressed by the Chinese word *yu* (幽) in the Chinese feminine ideal which makes or *ought* to make every *true* Chinese woman instinctively feel and know that it is wrong to show herself in public; that it is *indecent*, according to the Chinese idea, to go on a platform and sing before a crowd in the hall even of the Confucian Association. In fine, it is this *yu hsien* (幽閑), this love of seclusion, this sensitiveness against the "garish eye of day;" this *pudeur* in the Chinese feminine ideal, which gives to the true Chinese woman in China as to no other woman in the world,—a perfume, a perfume sweeter than the perfume of violets, the ineffable fragrance of orchids.

In the oldest love song, I believe, of the world, which I translated for the *Peking Daily News* two years ago—the first piece in the *Shih Ching* or Book of Poetry, the Chinese feminine ideal is thus described,

> *The birds are calling in the air,—*
> *An islet by the river-side;*
> *The maid is meek and debonair,*
> *Oh! Fit to be our Prince's bride.*

The words *yao t'iao* (窈窕) have the same signification as the words *yu sien* (幽閑) meaning literally *yao* (窈) secluded, meek, shy, and *t'iao* (窕) attractive, debonair, and the words *shu nu* (淑女) mean a pure, chaste girl or woman. Thus here in the oldest love song in China, you have the three essential qualities in the Chinese feminine ideal, viz. love of seclusion, bashfulness or *pudeur*, ineffable grace and charm expressed by the word debonair and last of all, purity or chastity. In short, the real or true Chinese woman is chaste; she is bashful, has *pudeur*; and she is attractive and debonair. This then is the Chinese feminine ideal,—the "Chinese Woman."

In the Confucian Catechism (中庸) which I have translated as

the Couduct of Life, the first part of the book containing the practical teaching of Confucius on the conduct of life concludes with the description of a Happy Home thus:

> " *When wife and children dwell in unison,*
> ' *Tis like to harp and lute well-played in tune,*
> *When brothers live in concord and in peace,*
> *The strain of harmony shall never cease.*
> *Make then your Home thus always gay and bright.*
> *Your wife and dear ones shall be your delight.*"

This Home in China is the miniature Heaven, —as the State with its civic order, the Chinese Empire, —is the real Heaven, the Kingdom of God come upon this earth, to the Chinese people. Thus, as the gentleman in China with his honour, his Religion of Loyalty is the guardian of the *State* the Civic Order, in China, so the Chinese woman, the Chinese gentlewoman or lady, with her debonair charm and grace, her purity, her pudeur, and above all, her Religion of Selflessness, —is the the Guardian Angel of the miniature Heaven, the *Home* in China.

THE CHINESE LANGUAGE

All foreigners who have tried to learn Chinese say that Chinese is a very difficult language. But is Chinese a difficult language? Before, however, we answer this question, let us understand what we mean by the Chinese language. There are, as everybody knows, two languages—I do not mean dialects, —in China, the spoken and the written language. Now, by the way, does anybody know the reason why the Chinese insist upon having these two distinct, spoken and written languages? I will here give you the reason. In China, as it was at one time in Europe when Latin was the learned or written language, the people are properly divided into two distinct classes, the educated and the uneducated. The colloquial or spoken language is the language for the use of the uneducated, and the written language is the language for the use of the really educated. In this way *half educated* people do not exist in this country. That is the reason, I say, why the Chinese insist upon having two languages. Now think of the consequences of having half educated people in a country. Look at Europe and America to-day. In Europe and America since, from the disuse of Latin, the sharp distinction between the spoken and the written language has disappeared, there has arisen a class of half educated people who are allowed to use the same language as the really educated people, who talk of civilisation, liberty, neutrality, militarism and panslavinism without in the least understanding what these words really mean. People say that Prussian Militarism is a danger to civilisation. But to me it seems, the half educated man, the mob of half educated men in the world to-day, is the real danger to civilisation. But that is neither here nor there.

Now to come to the question: is Chinese a difficult language? My answer is, yes and no. Let us first take the spoken language. The Chinese spoken language, I say, is not only *not* difficult, but as compared with the half dozen languages that I know, —the easiest language in the world except, —Malay. Spoken Chinese is easy because it is an extremely simple language. It is a language without case, without tense, without regular and irregular verbs; in fact without grammar, or any rule whatever. But people have said to me that Chinese is difficult even because of its simplicity; even because it has no rule or grammar. That, however, cannot be true. Malay like Chinese, is also a simple language without grammar or rules; and yet Europeans who learn it, do not find it difficult. Thus in itself and for the Chinese colloquial or spoken Chinese at least is not a difficult lauguage. But for educated Europeans and especially for half educated Europeans who come to China, even colloquial or spoken Chinese is a very difficult language: and why? Because spoken or colloquial Chinese is, as I said, the language of uneducated men, of thoroughly uneducated men; in fact the language of a child. Now as a proof of this, we all know how easily European children learn colloquial or spoken Chinese, while learned philogues and sinologues insist in saying that Chinese is so difficult. Chinese, colloquial Chinese, I say again is the language of a child. My first advice therefore to my foreign friends who want to learn Chinese is "Be ye like little children, you will then not only enter into the Kingdom of Heaven, but you will also be able to learn Chinese."

We now come to the written or book language, written Chinese. But here before I go further, let me say there are also different kinds of written Chinese. The Missionaries class these under two categories and call them easy *wen li* and difficult *wen li*. But that, in my opinion, is not a satisfactory classification. The proper classification, I think, should be, plain dress written Chinese; official uniform

Chinese; and full court dress Chinese. If you like to use Latin, call them: *litera communis or litera officinalis* (common or business Chinese); *litera classica minor* (lesser classical Chinese); and *litera classica major* (higher classical Chinese).

Now many foreigners have called themselves or have been called Chinese scholars. Writing an article on Chinese scholarship, some thirty years ago for the *N. C. Daily News*, —ah me! those old Shanghai days, *Tempora mutantur, nos et mutamur in illis*, —I then said: "Among Europeans in China, the publication of a few dialogues in some provincial *patois* or the collection of a hundred Chinese proverbs at once entitles a man to call himself a Chinese scholar." "There is, " I said, "of course no harm in a name, and with the extraterritoriality clause in the treaty, an Englishman in China may with impunity call himself Confucius, if so it pleases him. " Now what I want to say here is this: how many foreigners who call themselves Chinese scholars, have any idea of what an asset of civilisation is stored up in that portion of Chinese literature which I have called the *Classica majora*, the literature in full court dress Chinese? I say an asset of civilisation, because I believe that this *Classica majora* in the Chinese literature is something which can, as Matthew Arnold says of Homer's poetry, "refine the raw natural man: they can transmute him. " In fact, I believe this *Classica majora* in Chinese literature will be able to transform one day even the raw natural men who are now fighting in Europe as patriots, but with the fighting instincts of wild animals; transform them into peaceful, gentle and civil persons. Now the object of civilisation, as Ruskin says, is to make mankind into civil persons who will do away with coarseness, violence, brutality and fighting.

But *revenons à nos moutons*. Is then written Chinese a difficult language? My answer again is, yes and no. I say, written Chinese, even what I have called the full court dress Chinese, the *classica majora* Chinese, is not difficult, because, like the spoken or colloquial

Chinese, it is extremely simple. Allow me to show you by an average specimen taken at random how extremely simple, written Chinese even when dressed in full court dress uniform, is. The specimen I take is a poem of four lines from the poetry of the T'ang dynasty describing what sacrifices the Chinese people had to make in order to protect their civilisation against the wild half civilised fierce Huns from the North. The words of the poem in Chinese are:

誓扫匈奴不顾身

五千貂锦丧胡尘

可怜无定河边骨

犹是春闺梦里人

which translated into English word for word mean:

> Swear sweep the Huns not care self,
> Five thousand embroidery sable perish desert dust;
> Alas! Wuting riverside bones,
> Still are Spring chambers dream inside men!

A free English version of the poem is something like this:—

> They vowed to sweep the heathen hordes
> From off their native soil or die:
> Five thousand taselled knights, sable-clad,
> All dead now on the desert lie.
> Alas! the white bones that bleach cold
> Far off along the Wuting stream,
> Still come and go as living men
> Home somewhere in the loved one's dream.

Now, if you will compare it with my poor clumsy English version, you will see how plain in words and style, how simple in ideas, the original Chinese is. How plain and simple in words, style and ideas: and yet how *deep* in thought, how *deep* in feeling it is.

In order to have an idea of this kind of Chinese literature, —deep thought and deep feeling in extremely simple language, —you will have to read the Hebrew Bible. The Hebrew Bible is one of the deepest books in all the literature of the world and yet how plain and simple in language. Take this passage for instance: "How is this faithful city become a harlot! Thy men in the highest places are disloyal traitors and companions of thieves; every one loveth gifts and followeth after rewards; they judge not the fatherless neither doth the cause of the widow come before them." (Is. I 21-23), or this other passage from the same prophet: —"I will make children to be their high officials and babes shall rule over them. And the people shall be oppressed. The child shall behave himself proudly against the old man and the base against the honourable!" What a picture! The picture of the awful state of a nation or people. Do you see the picture before you now? In fact, if you want to have literature which can transmute men, can civilise mankind, you will have to go to the literature of the Hebrew people or of the Greeks or to Chinese literature. But Hebrew and Greek are now become dead languages, whereas Chinese is a living language—the language of four hundred million people still living to-day.

But now to sum up what I want to say on the Chinese language. Spoken as well as written Chinese is, in one sense, a very difficult language. It is difficult, not because it is complex. Many European languages such as Latin and French are difficult because they are complex and have many rules. Chinese is difficult not because it is complex, but because it is *deep*. It is difficult because it is a language for expressing deep feeling in simple language. That is the secret of the difficulty of the Chinese language. In fact, as I have said else where, Chinese is a language of the heart: a poetical language. That is the reason why even a simple letter in prose written in classical Chinese reads like poetry. In order to understand written Chinese, especially what I call full court dress Chinese, you must have your full nature, —the heart and the head, the soul and the intellect equally developed.

It is for this reason that for people with modern European education, Chinese is especially difficult, because modern European education developes principally only one part of a man's nature—his intellect. In other words, Chinese is difficult to a man with modern European education, because Chinese is a deep language and modern European education, which aims more at quantity than quality, is apt to make a man *shallow*. Finally for half educated people, even the spoken language, as I have said, is difficult. For half educated people it may be said of them as was once said of rich men, it is easier for a camel to go through the eye of a needle, than for them to understand high classical Chinese and for this reason: written Chinese is a language only for the use of *really educated* people. In short, written Chinese, classical Chinese is difficult because it is the language of really educated people and real education is a difficult thing but as the Greek proverb says, "all beautiful things are difficult."

But before I conclude, let me here give another specimen of written Chinese to illustrate what I mean by simplicity and depth of feeling which is to be found even in the *Classica Minora*, literature written in official uniform Chinese. It is a poem of four lines by a modern poet written on New Year's Eve. The words in Chinese are:

示　　内

莫道家资卒岁难
北风会过几番寒
明年桃柳堂前树
还汝春光满眼看

which, translated word for word, mean:—

Don't say home poor pass year hard,

North wind has blown many times cold ,
Next year peach willow hall front trees
Pay-back you spring light full eyes see .

A free translation would be something like this:

TO MY WIFE

Fret not , — though poor we yet can pass the year ;
Let the north wind blow ne' er so chill and drear ,
Next year when peach and willow are in bloom ,
You' ll yet see Spring and sunlight in our home .

Here is another specimen longer and more sustained. It is a poem by Tu Fu, the Wordsworth of China, of the T'ang Dynasty. I will here first give my English translation. The subject is

MEETING WITH AN OLD FRIEND

In life , friends seldom are brought near ;
Like stars , each one shines in its sphere .
To-night , — oh ! what a happy night !
We sit beneath the same lamplight .
Our youth and strength last but a day .
You and I — ah ! our hairs are grey .
Friends ! Half are in a better land ,
With tears we grasp each other' s hand .
Twenty more years , — short , after all ,
I once again ascend your hall .
When we met , you had not a wife ;
Now you have children , — such is life !
Beaming , they greet their father' s chum ;
They ask me from where I have come .
Before our say , we each have said ,
The table is already laid .
Fresh salads from the garden near ,

Rice mixed with millet, — frugal cheer.
When shall we meet? 'tis hard to know.
And so let the wine freely flow.
This wine, I know, will do no harm.
My old friend's welcome is so warm.
To-morrow I go, — to be whirled.
Again into the wide, wide world.

The above, my version I admit, is almost doggerel, which is meant merely to give the meaning of the Chinese text. But here is the Chinese text which is not doggerel, but *poetry* —poetry simple to the verge of colloquialism, yet with a grace, dignity pathos and *nobleness* which I cannot reproduce and which perhaps it is impossible to reproduce, in English in such simple language.

人生不相见　动如参与商
今夕复何夕　共此灯烛光
少壮能几时　须发各已苍
访旧半为鬼　惊呼热中肠
焉知二十载　重上君子堂
昔别君未婚　儿女忽成行
怡然敬父执　问我来何方
问答未及已　儿女罗酒浆
夜雨剪春韭　新炊间黄粱
主称会面难　一举累十觞
十觞亦不醉　感君故意长
明日隔山岳　世事两茫茫

JOHN SMITH IN CHINA

"The Philistine not only ignores all conditions of life which are not his own but he also demands that the rest of mankind should fashion its mode of existence after his own." * .... GOETHE.

Mr. W. Stead once asked: "What is the secret of Marie Corelli's popularity?" His answer was: "Like author, like reader; because the John Smiths who read her novels live in Marie Corelli's world and regard her as the most authoritative exponent of the Universe in which they live, move and have their being." What Marie Corelli is to the John Smiths in Great Britain, the Rev. Arthur Smith is to the John Smiths in China.

Now the difference between the really educated person and the half educated one is this. The really educated person wants to read books which will tell him the real truth about a thing, whereas the half educated person prefers to read books which will tell him what he wants the thing to be, what his vanity prompts him to wish that the thing should be. John Smith in China wants very much to be a superior person to the Chinaman and the Rev. Arthur Smith writes a book to prove conclusively that he, John Smith, is a very much superior person to the Chinaman. There-fore, the Rev. Arthur Smith is a person very dear to John Smith, and the "Chinese Characteristics" become a Bible to John Smith.

But Mr. W. Stead says, "It is John Smith and his neighbours who now rule the British Empire." Consequently I have lately taken the trouble to read the books which furnish John Smith with his ideas

---

* "Der Philister negiert nicht nur andere Zustande als der seininge ist, er will auch dass alle ubrigen Menschen auf seine Weise existieren sollen,"—GOETHE.

on China and the Chinese.

The Autocrat at the Breakfast Table classified minds under the heads of arithmetical and algebraical intellects. "All economical and practical wisdom," he observes, "is an extension or variation of the arithmetical formula 2 plus 2 equal 4. Every philosophical proposition has the more general character of the expression a plus b equal c." Now the whole family of John Smith belong decidedly to the category of minds which the Autocrat calls arithmetical intellects. John Smith's father, John Smith senr, alias John Bull, made his fortune with the simple formula 2 plus 2 equal 4. John Bull came to China to sell his Manchester goods and to make money and he got on very well with John Chinaman because both he and John Chinaman understood and agreed perfectly upon the formula 2 plus 2 equal 4. But John Smith Junr, who now rules the British Empire, comes out to China with his head filled with a plus b equal c which he does not understand—and not content to sell his Manchester goods, wants to civilise the Chinese or, as he expresses it, to "spread Anglo-Saxon ideals." The result is that John Smith gets on very badly with John Chinaman, and, what is still worse, under the civilising influence of John Smith's a plus b equal c Anglo-Saxon ideals, John Chinaman, instead of being a good, honest, steady customer for Manchester goods neglects his business, goes to Chang Su-ho's Gardens to celebrate the Constitution, in fact becomes a mad, raving reformer.

I have lately, by the help of Mr. Putnam Weale's "Reshaping of the Far East" and other books, tried to compile a Catechism of Anglo-Saxon Ideals for the use of Chinese students. The result, so far, is something like this:—

1. — What is the chief end of man?

The chief end of man is to glorify the British Empire.

2. —Do you believe in God?

Yes, when I go to Church.

3. — What do you believe in when you are not in Church?

I believe in interests—in what will pay.

4. —What is justification by faith?

To believe in everyone for himself.

5. —What is justification by works?

Put money in your pocket.

6. —What is Heaven?

Heaven means to be able to live in Bubbling Well Roa* and drive in victorias.

7. —What is Hell?

Hell means to be unsuccessful.

8. —What is a state of human perfectibility?

Sir Robert Hart's Custom Service in China.

9. —What is blasphemy?

To say that Sir Robert Hart is not a great man of genius.

10. —What is the most heinous sin?

To obstruct British trade.

11. —For what purpose did God create the four hundred million Chinese?

For the British to trade upon.

12. —What form of prayer do you use when you pray?

We thank Thee, O Lord, that we are not as the wicked Russians and brutal Germans are, who want to partition China.

13. —Who is the great Apostle of the Anglo-Saxon Ideals in China.

Dr. Morrison, the *Times* Correspondent in Peking.

It may be a libel to say that the above is a true statement of An-glo-Saxon ideals, but any one who will take the trouble to read Mr. Putnam Weale's book will not deny that the above is a fair represen-

---

* The most fashionable quarter in Shanghai.

tation of the Anglo-Saxon ideals of Mr. Putnam Weale and John Smith who reads Mr. Putnam Weale's books.

The most curious thing about the matter is that the civilising influence of John Smith's Anglo-Saxon ideals is really taking effect in China. Under this influence John Chinaman too is now wanting to glorify the Chinese Empire. The old Chinese literati with his eight-legged essays was a harmless humbug. But foreigners will find to their cost that the new Chinese literati who under the influence of John Smith's Anglo-Saxon ideals is clamouring for a constitution, is likely to become an intolerable and dangerous nuisance. In the end I fear John Bull Senior will not only find his Manchester goods trade ruined, but he will even be put to the expense of sending out a General Gordon or Lord Kitchener to shoot his poor old friend John Chinaman who has become *non compes mentis* under the civilising influence of John Smith's Anglo-Saxon ideals. But that is neither here nor there.

What I want to say here in plain, sober English is this. It is a wonder to me that the Englishman who comes out to China with his head filled with all the arrant nonsense written in books about the Chinese, can get along at all with the Chinese with whom he has to deal. Take this specimen, for instance, from a big volume, entitled "The Far East: its history and its questions," by Alexis Krausse.

"The crux of the whole question affecting the Powers of the Western nations in the Far East lies in the appreciation of the true inwardness of the Oriental mind. An Oriental not only sees things from a different standpoint to (!) the Occidental, but his whole train of thought and mode of reasoning are at variance. The very sense of perception implanted in the Asiatic varies from that with which we are endowed! "

After reading the last sentence an Englishman in China, when he wants a piece of *white* paper, if he follows the ungrammatical Mr.

Krausse's advice, would have to say to his boy:—"Boy, bring me a piece of *black* paper." It is, I think, to the credit of practical men among foreigners in China that they can put away all this nonsense about the true inwardness of the Oriental mind when they come to deal practically with the Chinese. In fact I believe that those foreigners get on best with the Chinese and are the most successful men in China who stick to 2 plus 2 equal 4, and leave the *a* plus *b* equal *c* theories of Oriental inwardness and Anglo-Saxon ideals to John Smith and Mr. Krausse. Indeed when one remembers that in those old days, before the Rev. Arthur Smith wrote his "Chinese Characteristics," the relations between the heads or taipans of great British firms such as Jardine, Matheson and their Chinese compradores * were always those of mutual affection, passing on to one or more generations; when one remembers this, one is inclined to ask what good, after all, has clever John Smith with his *a* plus *b* equal *c* theories of Oriental inwardness and Anglo-Saxon ideals done, either to Chinese or foreigners?

Is there then no truth in Kipling's famous dictum that East is East and West is West? Of course there is. When you deal with 2 plus 2 equal 4, there is little or no difference. It is only when you come to problems as *a* plus *b* equal *c* that there is a great deal of difference between East and West. But to be able to solve the equation *a* plus *b* equal *c* between East and West, one must have real aptitude for higher mathematics. The misfortune of the world to-day is that the solution of the equation *a* plus *b* equal *c* in Far Eastern problems, is in the hands of John Smith who not only rules the British Empire, but is an ally of the Japanese nation, —John Smith who does not understand the elements even of algebraical problems. The solu-

---

* Chinese employed by foreign firms in China to be agents between them and Chinese merchants.

tion of the equation a plus b equal c between East and West is a very complex and difficult problem. For in it there are many unknown quantities, not only such as the East of Confucius and the East of Mr. Kang Yu-wei and the Viceroy Tuan Fang, but also the West of Shakespeare and Goethe and the West of John Smith. Indeed when you have solved your *a* plus *b* equal *c* equation properly, you will find that there is very little difference between the East of Confucius and the West of Shakespeare and Goethe, but you will find a great deal of difference between even the West of Dr. Legge the scholar, and the West of the Rev. Arthur Smith. Let me give a concrete illustration of what I mean.

The Rev. Arthur Smith, speaking of Chinese histories, says: —

"Chinese histories are antediluvian, not merely in their attempts to go back to the ragged edge of zero of time for a point of departure, but in the interminable length of the sluggish and turbid current which carries on its bosom not only the mighty vegetation of past ages, but wood, hay and stubble past all reckoning. None but a relatively timeless race could either compose or read such histories: none but the Chinese memory could store them away in its capacious abdomen!"

Now let us hear Dr. Legge on the same subject. Dr. Legge, speaking of the 23 standard dynastic histories of China, says:

"No nation has a history so thoroughly digested; and on the whole it is trustworthy."

Speaking of another great Chinese literary collection, Dr. Legge says: — "The work was not published, as I once supposed by Imperial authority, but under the superintendence and at the expense (aided by other officers) of Yuen Yun, Governor-General of Kwangtung and Kwangse, in the 9th year of the last reign, of Kien-lung 1820. The publication of so extensive a work shows a *public spirit and zeal for literature* among the high officials of China which should keep foreigners from thinking meanly of them."

The above then is what I mean when I say that there is a great deal of difference not only between the East and West but also between the West of Dr. Legge, the scholar who can appreciate and admire zeal for literature, and the West of the Rev. Arthur Smith who is the beloved of John Smith in China.

A GREAT SINOLOGUE

Don't forget to be a gentleman of sense, while you try to be a great scholar;
Don't become a fool, while you try to be a great scholar.

Confucius Sayings, Ch: VI. II.

I have lately been reading Dr. Giles' "Adversaria Sinica," and in reading them, was reminded of a saying of another British consul Mr. Hopkins that "when foreign residents in China speak of a man as a sinologue, they generally think of him as a fool."

Dr. Giles' has the reputation of being a great Chinese scholar. Considering the quantity of work he has done, that reputation is not undeserved. But I think it is now time that an attempt should be made to accurately estimate the quality and real value of Dr. Giles' work.

In one respect Dr. Giles has the advantage over all sinologues past and present, —he possesses the literary gift: he can write good idiomatic English. But on the other hand Dr. Giles utterly lacks the philosophical insight and sometimes even common sense. He can translate Chinese sentences, but he cannot interpret and understand Chinese thought. In this respect, Dr. Giles has the same characteristics as the Chinese literati. Confucius says, "When men's education or book learning get the better of their natural qualities, they become *literati*." (Chap. VI. 16.)

To the Chinese literati, books and literature are merely materials for writing books and so they write books upon books. They live, move and have their being in a world of books, having nothing to do with the world of real human life. It never occurs to the literati that books and literature are only means to an end. The study of books and literature to the true scholar is but the means to enable him to interpret, to criticise, to understand human life.

Matthew Arnold says, "It is through the apprehension either of all literature, — the entire history of the human spirit, — or of a single great literary work as a connected whole, that the power of literature makes itself felt." But in all that Dr. Giles has written, there is not a single sentence which betrays the fact that Dr. Giles has conceived or even tried to conceive the Chinese literature as a connected whole.

It is this want of philosophical insight in Dr. Giles which makes him so helpless in the arrangement of his materials in his books. Take for instance his great dictionary. It is in no sense a dictionary at all. It is merely a collection of Chinese phrases and sentences, translated by Dr. Giles without any attempt at selection, arrangement, order or method. As a dictionary for the purposes of the scholar, Dr. Giles' dictionary is decidedly of less value than even the old dictionary of Dr. Williams.

Dr. Giles' Chinese biographical dictionary, it must be admitted, is a work of immense labour. But here again Dr. Giles shows an utter lack of the most ordinary judgment. In such a work, one would expect to find notices only of really notable men.

> *Hic manus ob patriam pugnando vulnera passi,*
> *Quique sacerdotes casti, dum vita manebat,*
> *Quique pii vates et Phoebo digna locuti,*
> *Inventas aut qui vitam excoluere per artes,*
> *Quique sui memores aliquos fecere merendo.* *

But side by side with sages and heroes of antiquity, with mythical and mythological personages, we find General Tcheng Ki-tong,

---

* 这里有一群为祖国在战争中受伤的人
  另一些在世时则是圣洁的祭司,
  有的是虔诚的诗人,说出无愧于费布思之言,
  有的是富于创新精神的,使生活丰富多彩的艺术家,
  还有些人留下了使人们怀念的业绩。

Mr. Ku Hung-ming, Viceroy Chang Chi-tung and Captain Lew Buah, —the last whose sole title to distinction is that he used often to treat his foreign friends with unlimited quantities of champagne!

Lastly these "Adversaria,"—Dr. Giles' latest publication—will not, I am afraid, enhance Dr. Giles' reputation as a scholar of sense and judgment. The subjects chosen, for the most part, have no earthly practical or human interest. It would really seem that Dr. Giles has taken the trouble to write these books not with any intention to tell the world anything about the Chinese and their literature but to show what a learned Chinese scholar Dr. Giles is and how much better he understands Chinese than anybody else. Moreover, Dr. Giles, here as elsewhere, shows a harsh and pugnacious dogmatism which is as un-philosophical, as unbecoming a scholar as it is unpleasing. It is these characteristics of sinologues like Dr. Giles which have made, as Mr. Hopkins says, the very name of sinologue and Chinese scholarship a byword and scorn among practical foreign residents in the Far East.

I shall here select two articles from Dr. Giles' latest publication and will try to show that if hitherto writings of foreign scholars on the subjects of Chinese learning and Chinese literature have been without human or practical interest, the fault is not in Chinese learn-ing and Chinese literature.

The first article is entitled "What is filial piety." The point in the article turns upon the meaning of two Chinese characters. A disci-ple asked what is filial piety. Confucius said: *se nan* 色难 (lit, colour difficult).

Dr. Giles says, "The question is, and has been for twenty cen-turies past, what do these two characters mean?" After citing and dis-missing all the interpretations and translations of native and foreign scholars alike, Dr. Giles of course finds out the true meaning. In order to show Dr. Giles harsh and unscholarly dogmatic manner, I shall here quote Dr. Giles' words with which he announces his discovery. Dr.

Giles says:—

"It may seem presumptuous after the above exordium to declare that the meaning lies à la Bill Stumps (!) upon the surface, and all you have to do, as the poet says, is to

Stoop, and there it is;

Seek it not right nor left!

"When Tzu-hsia asked Confucius, 'What is filial piety?' the latter replied simply,

"'*se* (色) to define it, nan (难) is difficult,' a most intelligible and appropriate answer."

I shall not here enter into the niceties of Chinese grammar to show that Dr. Giles is wrong. I will only say here that if Dr. Giles is right in supposing that the character *se* (色) is a verb, then in good grammatical Chinese, the sentence would not read *se nan* (色难), but *se chih wei nan* (色之维难) to define it, is difficult. The impersonal pronoun *chih* (之) *it*, is here absolutely indispensable, if the character *se* (色) here is used as a verb.

But apart from grammatical niceties, the translation as given by Dr. Giles of Confucius answer, when taken with the whole context, has no point or sense in it at all.

Tzu hsia asked, what is filial piety? Confucius said, "The difficulty is with the *manner* * of doing it. That merely when there is work to be done, the young people should take the trouble of doing it, and when there is wine and food, the old folk are allowed to partake it,—do you really think that is filial piety?" (Discourses and Sayings Ch. II. 9.) Now the whole point in the text above lies in this,—that importance is laid not upon what duties you perform towards your parents, but upon *how* —in what manner, with what spirit, you per-

---

* Compare another saying of Confucius 巧言令色 *Ch' iao yen ling se*, plausible speech and fine *manners* (Discourses and Sayings Ch. I. 3.)

form those duties.

The greatness and true efficacy of Confucius' moral teaching, I wish to say here, lies in this very point which Dr. Giles fails to see, — the point namely that in the performance of moral duties, Confucius insisted upon the importance not of the *what*, but of the *how*. For herein lies the difference between what is called morality and religion, between mere rules of moral conduct and the vivifying teaching of great and true religious teachers. Teachers of morality merely tell you what kind of action is moral and what kind of action is immoral. But true religious teachers do not merely tell you this. True religious teachers do not merely inculcate the doing of the outward act, but insist upon the importance of the manner, the *inwardness* of the act. True religious teachers teach that the morality or immorality of our actions does not consist in *what* we do, but in *how* we do it.

This is what Matthew Arnold calls Christ's method in his teaching. When the poor widow gave her mite, it was not *what* she gave that Christ called the attention of his hearers to, but *how* she gave it. The moralists said, "Thou shalt not commit adultery." But Christ said, "I say unto you that whosoever looketh on a woman to lust after her hath already committed adultery."

In the same way the moralists in Confucius' time said: Children must cut firewood and carry water for their parents and yield to them the best of the food and wine in the house: that is filial peity. But Confucius said, "No; that is *not* filial piety." True filial piety does not consist in the mere outward performance of these services to our parents. True filial piety coonsists in *how*, in what manner, with what spirit we perform these services. The difficulty, said Confucius, is with the *manner* of doing it. It is, I will finally say here, by virtue of this method in his teaching, of looking into the inwardness of moral actions that Confucius becomes, not as the Christian missionaries say, a mere moralist and philosopher, but a great and true religious teacher.

As a further illustration of Confucius method, take the present reform movement in China. The so-called progressive mandarins with applause from foreign newspapers are making a great fuss—even going to Europe and America,—trying to find out what reforms to adopt in China. But unfortunately the salvation of China will not depend upon *what* reforms are made by these progressive mandarins, but upon *how* these reforms are carried out. It seems a pity that these progressive mandarins,—instead of going to Europe and America, to study constitution could not be made to stay at home and study Confucius. For until these mandarins take to heart Confucius' teaching and his method-and attend to the *how* instead of the *what* in this matter of reform, nothing but chaos, misery and suffering will come out of the present reform movement in China.

The other article in Dr. Giles "Adversaria Sinica" which I will briefly examine, is entitled— "The four classes."

The Japanese Baron Suyematsu in an interview said that the Japanese divided their people into four classes,—soldiers, farmers, artisans and warriors. Upon this Dr. Giles says. "It is incorrect to translate *shih* (士) as soldier; that is a later meaning." Dr. Giles further says, "in its earliest use the word *shih* (士) referred to civilians."

Now the truth is just on the other side. In its earliest use, the word *shih* (士) referred to gentlemen who in ancient China, as it is now in Europe, bore arms,—the *noblesse* of the sword. Hence the officers and soldiers of an army were spoken of as *shih tsu* (士卒).

The civilian official class in ancient China were called *shi* (史)—clericus. When the feudal system in China was abolished (2nd cent. B.C.,) and fighting ceased to be the only profession of gentlemen, this civilian official class rose into prominence, became lawyers and constituted the *noblesse* of the robe as distinguished from the *shih* (士) the *noblesse* of the sword.

H.E. the Viceroy Chang of Wuchang once asked me why the

foreign consuls who were civil functionaries, when in full dress, wore swords. In reply I said that it was because they were *shih* (士) which in ancient China meant not a civilian scholar, but a gentleman who bore arms and served in the army. H. E. agreed and the next day gave orders that all the pupils in the schools in Wuchang should wear military uniform.

This question therefore which Dr. Giles has raised whether the Chinese word *shih* (士) means a civilian or a military man has a great practical interest. For the question whether China in the future will be independent or come under a foreign yoke will depend upon whether she will ever have an efficient army and that question again will depend upon whether the educated and governing class in China will ever regain the true ancient meaning and conception of the word *shih* (士) not as civilian scholar, but as a gentleman who bears arms and is able to defend his country against aggression.

CHINESE SCHOLARSHIP

PART I

Not long ago a body of missionaries created a great deal of amusement by styling themselves, on the cover of some scientific tracts, as "famous savants" *su ju* (宿儒). The idea was of course extremely ridiculous. There is certainly not one Chinaman in the whole Empire who would venture to arrogate to himself the Chinese word *ju*, which includes in it all the highest attributes of a scholar or literary man. We often hear, however, a European spoken of as a Chinese scholar. In the advertisement of the *China Review*, we are told that "among the missionaries a high degree of Chinese scholarship is assiduously cultivated." A list is then given of regular contributors, "all," we are to believe, "well-known names, indicative of sound scholarship and thorough mastery of their subject."

Now in order to estimate the high degree of scholarship said to be assiduously cultivated by the missionary bodies in China, it is not necessary to take such high ideal standards as those propounded by the German Fichte in his lectures upon the Literary Man, or the American Emerson in his Literary Ethics. The late American Minister to Germany, Mr. Taylor, was acknowledged to be a great German scholar; but though an Englishman who has read a few plays of Schiller, or sent to a magazine some verses translated from Heine, might be thought a German scholar among his tea drinking circles, he would scarcely have his name appear as such in print or placard. Yet among Europeans in China the publication of a few dialogues in some provincial *patois*, or collection of a hundred proverbs, at once entitles a mán to be called a Chinese scholar. There is, of course, no harm in a name, and, with the exterritorial clause in the treaty, an Englishman in China might with impunity call himself Confucius if so it pleases him.

We have been led to consider this question because it is thought by some that Chinese scholarship has passed, or is passing, the early pioneering, and is about to enter a new stage, when students of Chinese will not be content with dictionary-compiling or such other brick-carrying work, but attempts will be made at works of construction, at translations of the most perfect specimens of the national literature, and not only judgment, but final judgment, supported with reasons and arguments, be passed upon the most venerated names of the Chinese literary Pantheon. We now propose to examine: 1st, how far it is true that the knowledge of Chinese among Europeans is undergoing this change; 2ndly, what has already been done in Chinese scholarship; 3rdly, what is the actual state of Chinese scholarship at the present day; and in the last place, to point out what we conceive Chinese scholarship should be. It has been said that a dwarf standing upon the shoulders of a giant is apt to imagine himself of greater dimensions than the giant; still, it must be admitted that the dwarf, with the advantage of his position, will certainly command a wider and more extensive view. We will, therefore, standing upon the shoulders of those who have preceded us, take a survey of the past, present, and future of Chinese scholarship; and if, in our attempt, we should be led to express opinions not wholly of approval of those who have gone before us, these opinions, we hope, may not be construed to imply that we in any way plume ourselves upon our superiority: we claim only the advantage of our position.

First, then, that the knowledge of Chinese among Europeans has changed, is only so far true, it seems to us, that the greater part of the difficulty of acquiring a knowledge of the language has been removed.

"The once prevalent belief," says Mr. Giles, "in the great difficulty of acquiring a colloquial knowledge, even of a single Chinese dialect has long since taken its place among other historical fictions." Indeed, even with regard to the written language, a student in the British Consular Service, after two years' residence in Peking and a year or two at a Consulate, can now readily make out at sight the general meaning of an ordinary despatch. That the knowledge of Chinese among foreigners in China has so far changed, we readily admit; but what is contended for beyond this we feel very much inclined to doubt.

After the early Jesuit missionaries, the publication of Dr. Morrison's famous dictionary is justly regarded as the *point de départ* of all that has been accomplished in Chinese scholarship. The work will certainly remain a standing monument of the earnestness, zeal and conscientiousness of the early Protestant Missionaries. After Morrison came a class of scholars of whom Sir John Davis and Dr. Gutzlaff might be taken as representatives. Sir John Davis really knew no Chinese, and he was honest enough to confess it himself. He certainly spoke Mandarin and could perhaps without much difficulty read a novel written in that dialect. But such knowledge as he then possessed, would now-a-days scarcely qualify a man for an interpretership in any of the Consulates. It is nevertheless very remarkable that the notions about the Chinese of most Englishmen, even to this day, will be found to have been acquired from Sir John Davis's book on China. Dr. Gutzlaff perhaps knew a little more Chinese than Sir John Davis; but he attempted to pass himself off as knowing a great deal more than he did. The late Mr. Thomas Meadows afterwards did good service in exposing the pretension of Dr. Gutzlaff, and such other men as the missionaries Huc and Du Halde. After this, it is curious to find Mr. Boulger, in his recent History of China, quoting these men as authorities.

In France, Rémusat was the first to occupy a Chair of Chinese Professorship in any European University. Of his labours we are not in a position to express an opinion. But one book of his attracted notice: it was a translation of a novel, "The Two Cousins." The book was read by Leigh Hunt, and by him recommended to Carlyle, and by Carlyle to John Stirling, who read it with delight, and said that the book was certainly written by a man of genius, but "a man of genius after the dragon pattern." the *Ju Kiao Li*, * as the novel is called in Chinese, is a pleasant enough book to read, but it takes no high place even among the inferior class of books of which it is a specimen. Nevertheless it is always pleasant to think that thoughts and images from the brain of a Chinaman have actually passed through such minds as those of Carlyle and Leigh Hunt.

After Rémusat followed Stanislas Julien and Pauthier. The German poet Heine says that Julien made the wonderful and important discovery that Mons. Pauthier did not understand Chinese at all and the latter, on the other hand, also made a discovery, namely that Monsieur Julien knew no Sanscrit. Nevertheless the pioneering work done by these writers was very considerable. One advantage they possessed was that they were thorough masters of their own language. Another French writer might be mentioned, Mons. D'Harvey St. Denys, whose translation of the T'ang poets is a breach made into one department of Chinese literature in which nothing has been done before or since.

In Germany Dr. Plath of Munich published a book on China, which he entitled "Die Manchurei." Like all books written in Germany, it is a solid piece of work thoroughly well done. Its evident design was to give a history of the origin of the present Manchu dynasty in China. But the latter portions of the book contain information on

---

* 玉娇梨

questions connected with China, which we know not where to find in any other book written in a European language. Such work as Dr. Williams's Middle Kingdom is a mere nursery story-book compared with it. Another German Chinese scholar is Herr von Strauss, formerly the Minister of a little German principality which has since 1866 been swallowed up by Prussia. The old Minister in his retirement amused himself with the study of Chinese. He published a translation of Lao Tzu, and recently of the Shih King. Mr. Faber, of Canton, speaks of some portions of his Lao Tzu as being perfect. His translation of the Odes is also said to be very spirited. We have, unfortunately, not been able to procure these books.

The scholars we have named above may be regarded as sinologues of the earliest period, beginning with the publication of Dr. Morrisons's dictionary. The second period began with the appearance of two standard works: 1st, the Tzu Erh Chih of Sir Thomas Wade; 2nd, the Chinese Classics of Dr. Legge.

As to the first, those who have now gone beyond the Mandarin colloquial in their knowledge might be inclined to regard it lightly. But it is, notwithstanding, a great work—the most perfect, within the limits of what was attempted, of all the English books that have been published on the Chinese language. The book, moreover, was written in response to a crying necessity of the time. Some such book had to be written, and lo! it was done, and done in a way that took away all chance of contemporary as well as future competition.

That the work of translating the Chinese Classics had to be done, was also a necessity of the time, and Dr. Legge has accomplished it, and the result is a dozen huge, ponderous tomes. The quantity of work done is certainly stupendous, whatever may be thought of the quality. In presence of these huge volumes we feel almost afraid to speak. Nevertheless, it must be confessed that the work does not altogether satisfy us. Mr. Balfour justly remarks that in translating these classics a great deal depends upon the *terminology* employed by the translator. Now we feel that the terminology employed by Dr. Legge is harsh, crude, inadequate, and in some places, almost unidiomatic. So far for the form. As to the matter, we will not hazard our own opinion, but will let the Rev. Mr. Faber of Canton speak for us. "Dr. Legge's own notes on Mencius," he says, "show that Dr. Legge has not a philosophic understanding of his author." We are certain that Dr. Legge could not have read and translated these works without having in some way tried to conceive and shape to his own mind the teaching of Confucius and his school as a connected whole; yet it is extraordinary that neither in his notes nor in his dissertations has Dr. Legge let slip a single phrase or sentence to show what he conceived the teaching of Confucius really to be, as a philosophic whole. Altogether, therefore, Dr. Legge's judgment on the value of these works cannot by any means be accepted as final, and the translator of the Chinese Classics is yet to come. Since the appearance of the two works above mentioned, many books have been written on China: a few, it is true, of really great scholastic importance; but none, we believe showing that Chinese scholarship has reached an important turning point.

First, there is Mr. Wylie's "Notes on Chinese Literature." It is, however, a mere catalogue, and not a book with any literary pretension at all. Another is the late Mr. Mayers's "Chinese Readers Manual." It is certainly not a work that can lay claim to any degree of perfection. Nevertheless, it is a very great work, the most honest conscientious and unpretending of all the books that have been written on China. Its usefulness, moreover, is inferior only to the Tzu-Erh-Chi of Sir Thomas Wade.

Another Chinese scholar of note is Mr. Herbert A. Giles of the British Consular Service. Like the early French sinologues, Mr. Giles possesses the enviable advantage of a clear, vigorous, and beautiful

style. Every object he touches upon becomes at once clear and lumi-
nous. But with one or two exceptions, he has not been quite fortunate
in the choice of subjects worthy of his pen. One exception is the
"Strange Stories from a Chinese Studio," which may be taken as a
model of what translation from the Chinese should be. But the *Liao-
chai-chih-i*, a remarkably beautiful literary work of art though it be,
belongs yet not to the highest specimens of Chinese literature.

Next to Dr. Legge's labours, Mr. Balfour's recent translation of
the Nan-hua King of Chuang-tzu is a work of certainly the highest
ambition. We confess to have experienced, when we first heard the
work announced, a degree of expectation and delight which the an-
nouncement of an Englishman entering the Hanlin College would
scarcely have raised in us. The Nan-hua King is acknowledged by the
Chinese to be one of the most perfect of the highest specimens of their
national literature. Since its appearance two centuries before the
Christian era, the influence of the book upon the literature of China is
scarcely inferior to the works of Confucius and his schools; while its
effect upon the language and spirit of the poetical and imaginative literature of succeeding dynasties is almost as exclusive as that of the
Four Books and Five Chinese upon the philosophical works of China.
But Mr. Balfour's work is not a translation at all; it is simply a *mis-
translation*. This, we acknowledge, is a heavy, and for us, daring
judgment to pass upon a work upon which Mr. Balfour must have
spent many years. But we have ventured it, and it will be expected of
us to make good our judgment. We believe Mr. Balfour would hardly
condesend to join issue with us if we were to raise the question of the
true interpretation of the philosophy of Chuang-tzu. "But,"—we
quote from the Chinese preface of Lin Hsi-chung, a recent editor of
the Nan-hua King—"in reading a book, it is necessary to understand
first the meaning of each single word: then only can you construe the
sentences, then only can you perceive the arrangement of the para-

graphs; and then, last of all, can you get at the central proposition of the whole chapter." Now every page of Mr. Balfour's translation bears marks that he has not understood the meaning of many single words, that he has not construed the sentences correctly, and that he has missed the arrangement of the paragraphs. If these propositions which we have assumed can be proved to be true, as they can easily be done, being merely points regarding rules of grammar and syntax, it then follows very clearly that Mr. Balfour has missed the meaning and central proposition of whole chapters.

But of all the Chinese scholars of the present day we are inclined to place the Reverend Mr. Faber of Canton at the head. We do not think that Mr. Faber's labours are of more scholastic value or a higher degree of literary merit than the works of others, but we find that almost every sentence he has written shows a grasp of literary and philosophic principles such as we do not find in any other scholar of the present time. What we conceive these principles to be we must reserve for the next portion of the present paper, when we hope to be able to state the methods, aims, and objects of Chinese scholarship.

CHINESE SCHOLARSHIP

PART II

Mr. Faber has made the remark that the Chinese do not understand any systematic method of scientific enquiry. Nevertheless in one of Chinese Classics, called "Higher Education*," a work which is considered by most foreign scholars as a Book of Platitudes, a concatenation is given of the order in which the systematic study of a scholar should be pursued. The student of Chinese cannot perhaps do better than follow the course laid down in that book namely, to begin his study with the individual, to proceed from the individual to the family, and from the family to the Government.

First, then: it is necessary and indispensable that the student should endeavour to arrive at a just knowledge of the principles of individual conduct of the Chinese. Secondly, he will examine and see how these principles are applied and carried out in the complex social relations and family life of the people. Thirdly, he will be able then to give his attention, and direct his study, to the government and administrative institutions of the country. Such a programme as we have indicated, can, of course, be followed out only in general outline; to carry it fully out would require the devotion and undivided energies of almost a whole lifetime. But we should certainly refuse to consider a man, a Chinese scholar or a attribute to him any high degree of scholarship, unless he had in some way made himself familiar with the principles above indicated. The German poet Goethe says: "In the

---

* Known among foreigners as the "Great Learning".

works of man, as in those of nature, what is really deserving of attention, above everything, is—the *intention*." Now in the study of national character, it is also of the first importance to pay attention, not
only to the actions and practice of the people, but also to their notions
and theories; to get a knowledge of what they consider as good and
what as bad, what they regard as just and what as unjust, what they
look upon as beautiful and what as not beautiful, and how they distinguish wisdom from foolishness. This is what we mean when we say
that the student of Chinese should study the principles of individual
conduct. In other words, we mean to say that you must get at the *national ideals*. If it is asked how this is to be attained: we answer, by
the study of the national literature, in which revelations of the best
and highest as well as the worst side of the character of a people can
be read. The one object, therefore, which should engage the attention
of the foreign student of Chinese, is the standard national literature of
the people: whatever preparatory studies it may by necessary for him
to go through should serve only as means towards the attainment of
that one object. Let us now see how the student is to study the Chinese literature.

"The civilisations of Europe," says a German writer, "rest upon
those of Greece, Rome and Palestine; the Indians and Persians are of
the same Aryan stock as the people of Europe, and are therefore relat-
ed; and the influence of the intercourse with the Arabs during the
Middle Ages, upon European culture has not even to this day, altogether disappeared." But as for the Chinese, the origin and development of their civilisation rest upon foundations altogether foreign to
the culture of the people of Europe. The foreign student of Chinese
literature, therefore, has all the disadvantages to overcome which must
result form the want of community of primary ideas and notions. It
will be necessary for him, not only to equip himself with these foreign
notions and ideas, but also, first of all, to find their equivalents in the

Europe languages, and if these equivalents do not exist, to disintegrate them, and to see to which side of the universal nature of man these ideas and notions may be referred. Take, for instance, those Chinese words of constant recurrence in the Classics, and generally translated into English as "benevolence," (仁) "justice," (义) and "propriety" (礼). Now when we come to take these English words together with the context, we feel that they are not adequate: they do not connote all the ideas the Chinese words contain. Again, the word "humanity," is perhaps the most exact equivalent for the Chinese word translated "benevolence;" but then, "humanity" must be understood in a sense different from its idiomatic use in the English language. A venturesome translator would use the "love" and "righteousness" of the Bible, which are perhaps as exact as any other, having regard both for the sense of the words and the idiom of the language. Now, however, if we disintegrate and refer the primary notions which these words convey, to the universal nature of man, we get, at once, at their full significance: namely, "the good," "the true," and "the beautiful."

But, moreover, the literature of a nation, if it is to be studied at all, must be studied systematically and as one connected whole, and not fragmentarily and without plan or order, as it has hitherto been done by most foreign scholars. "It is," says Mr. Matthew Arnold, "it is through the apprehension, either of all literature, —the entire history of the human spirit, —or of a single great literary work, as a connected whole that the real power of literature makes itself felt." Now how little, we have seen, do the foreign students conceive the Chinese literature as a whole! How little, therefore, do they get at its significance! How little, in fact, do they know it! How little does it become a power in their hands, towards the understanding of the character of the people! With the exception of the labours of Dr. Legge and of one or two other scholars, the people of Europe know of the Chinese literature principally through the translations of novels, and even these not of the best, but of the most commonplace of their class. Just fancy, if a foreigner were to judge of the English literature from the works of Miss Rhoda Broughton, or that class of novels which form the reading stock of school-boys and nursery-maids! It was this class of Chinese literature which Sir Thomas Wade must have had in his mind, when in his wrath he reproached the Chinese with "tenuity of intellect."

Another extraordinary judgment which used to be passed upon Chinese literature was, that it was excessively over-moral. Thus the Chinese people were actually accused of over morality, while at the same time most foreigners are pretty well agreed that the Chinese are a nation of liars! But we can now explain this by the fact that, besides the trashy novels we have already noticed, the work of translation a-mong students of Chinese was formerly confined exclusively to the Confucian Classics. Nevertheless, there are of course a great many other things in these writings besides morality, and, with all deference to Mr. Balfour, we think that "the admirable doctrines" these books contain are decidedly not "utilitarian and worldly" as they have been judged to be. We will just submit two sentences and ask Mr. Balfour if he really thinks them "utilitarian and mundane." "He who sins against Heaven," said Confucius in answer to a Minister, "he who sins against Heaven has no place where he can turn to and pray." Again, Mencius says: "I love life, but I also love righteousness: but if I cannot keep them both, I would give up life and choose righteous-ness."

We have thought it worthwhile to digress so far in order to protest against Mr. Balfour's judgment, because we think that such smart phrases as "a bondslave to antiquity," "a past-master in casu-istry" should scarcely be employed in a work purposely philosophical, much less applied to the most venerated name in China. Mr. Balfour was probably led astray by his admiration of the Prophet of Nan-hua, and, in his eagerness to emphasize the superiority of the Taoist over the orthodox school, he has been betrayed into the use of expressions which, we are sure, his calmer judgment must condemn.

But to return from our digression. We have said that the Chinese literature must be studied as a connected whole. Moreover we have noted that the people of Europe are accustomed to conceive and form their judgment of the literature of China solely from those writings with which the name of Confucius is associated; but, in fact, the literary activity of the Chinese had only just begun with the labours of Confucius, and has since continued through eighteen dynasties, including more than two thousand years. At the time of Confucius, the literary form of writing was still very imperfectly understood.

Here let us remark that, in the study of a literature, there is one important point to be attended to, but which has hitherto been completely lost sight of by foreign students of Chinese; namely, the *form* of the literary writings. "To be sure," said the poet Wordsworth, "it was the matter, but then you know the *matter* always comes out of the *manner*." Now it is true that the early writings with which the name of Confucius is associated do not pretend to any degree of perfection, as far as the literary form is concerned: they are considered as classical or standard works not so much for their classical elegance of style or perfection of literary form, as for the value of the matter they contain. The father of Su Tung-po, of the Sung dynasty, remarks that something approaching to the formation of a prose style may be traced in the dialogues of Mencius. Nevertheless Chinese literary writings, both in prose and poetry, have since been developed into many forms and styles. The writings of the Western Hans, for instance, differ from the essays of the Sung period, much in the same way as the prose of Lord Bacon is different from the prose of Addison or Goldsmith. The wild exaggeration and harsh diction of the poetry of the six dynasties are as unlike the purity, vigour, and brilliancy of the T' ang poets as the early weak and immature manner of Keats is unlike the strong, clear, and correct splendour of Tennyson.

Having thus, as we have shown, equipped himself with the primary principles and notions of the people, the student will then be in a position to direct his study to the social relations of the people; to see how these principles are applied and carried out. But the social institutions, manners and customs of a people do not grow up, like mushrooms, in a night, but are developed and formed into what they are, through long centuries. It is therefore necessary to study the history of the people. Now the history of the Chinese people is as yet almost unknown to European scholars. The so-called History of China, by Mr. Demetrius Boulger, published recently, is perhaps the worst history that could have been written of a civilised people like the Chinese. Such a history as Mr. Boulger has written might be tolerated if written of some such savage people as the Hottentots. The very fact that such a history of China could have been published, serves only to show how very far from being perfect yet is the knowledge of Chinese among Europeans. Without a knowledge of their history, therefore, no correct judgment can be formed of the social institutions of a people. Such works as Dr. Williams's *Middle Kingdom* and other works on China from want of such knowledge, are not only useless for the purpose of the scholar, but are even misleading for the mass of general readers. Just to take one instance, —the social ceremony of the people. The Chinese are certainly a ceremonious people, and it is true that they owe this to the influence of the teaching of Confucius. Now Mr. Balfour may speak of the pettifogging observances of a ceremonial life as much as he pleases; nevertheless, even "the bows and scrapes of external decorum, " as Mr. Giles calls them, have their roots deep in the universal nature of man, in that side of human nature, namely, which we have defined as the sense of the beautiful. "In the use of ceremony, " says a disciple of Confucius, "what is important, is to be natural; this is what is really beautiful in the ways of the ancient Emperors." Again, it is said somewhere in the Classics: "Ceremony is simply the expression of reverence." (the *Ehrfürcht* of Goethe's *Wilk elm Meister*) We now see how evident it is that a judgment of the manners and customs of a nation should be founded upon the knowledge of the moral principles of the people. Moreover the study, of the Government and political institutions of a country, —which, we have said should be reserved by the student to the last stage of his labours, —must also be founded upon an understanding of their philosophical principles and a knowledge of their history.

We will conclude with a quotation from "The Higher Education," or the Book of Platitudes, as foreigners consider it. "The Government of the Empire," it is said in that book, "should begin with the proper administration of the State; the administration of the State begins with the regulation of the family; the regulation of the family begins with the cultivation of the individual." This, then, is what we mean by Chinese Scholarship.

This article on Chinese Scholarship was written and published in the "N. C. DAILY NEWS" in Shanghai in 1884.

APPENDIX

The Religion of Mob-Worship
OR
The War and The Way Out

Frankreich's traurig Geschick, die Grossen mögen's bedenken,
Aber bedenken fürwahr sollen es Kleine nech mehr;
Grossen gingen zu Grunde; doch wer beschütze die Menge
Gegen die Menge? Da war Menge der Menge Tyrann. *

Goethe

Professor Lowes Dickinson of Cambridge University in an eloquent passage of his article on "The War and the Way out," says: "The future (the future of civilisation in Europe, he means) cannot be moulded to any purpose until the plain men and women, workers with their hands and workers with their brains in England and in Germany and in all countries get together and say to the people who have led them into this catastrophe and will lead them into such again and again, "No more! No more! And never again! you rulers, soldiers and diplomats, you who through the long agony of history have conducted the destinies of mankind and conducted them to hell, we do now repudiate you. Our labour and our blood have been at your disposal. They shall be so no more. You shall not make the peace as you have made the war. The Europe that shall come out of this war shall be *our* Europe. And it shall be one in which another European

---

* Dreadful is France's misfortune, the Classes should truly bethink them,
    But still more of a truth, the Masses should lay it to heart.
  Classes were smashed up; well then, but who will protect now the Masses
    'Gainst the Masses? Against the Masses the Masses did rage.

war shall be never possible."

That is the dream of the socialists now in Europe. But such a dream, I am afraid, can never be realised. When the plain men and women in the countries of Europe get rid of the rulers, soldiers and diplomats and take into their own hands the question of peace and war with another country, I am perfectly sure, before that very question is decided, there will be quarrels, broken heads and wars between the plain men and women themselves in every country. Take the case of the Irish question in Great Britain. The plain men and women in Ireland in trying to take into their own hands the question even of how to govern themselves were actually flying at each others' throats and if this greater war had not come, would at this moment, be cutting each other's throats.

Now in order to find a way out of this war, we must first of all, find out the origin, the cause of this war; find out who was really responsible for this war. Professor Dickinson would have us believe that it was the rulers, soldiers and diplomats who have led the plain men and women into this catastrophe, —into this hell of a war. But I think, I can prove, that it was not the rulers, soldiers and diplomats who have led the plain men and women into this war, but it was the plain men and women who have driven and pushed the poor helpless rulers, soldiers and diplomats of Europe into this hell of a war.

Let us first take the case of the actual rulers, —the Emperors, Kings and Presidents of Republic now in Europe. Now it is an undisputed fact that with the exception perhaps of the Emperor of Germany, the actual rulers of the countries now at war have had no say whatever in the making of this war. In fact the actual rulers of Europe today, Emperors, Kings and Presidents, bound in hand and foot and gagged by the mouth as they all are by Constitutions and Magna Chartas of Liberty, —these actual rulers have no say whatever in the government or conduct of public affairs in their countries. Poor King

George of Great Britain, when he tried to say something to prevent a civil war over the Irish question, was peremptorily told by the plain men and women in Great Britain to hold his tongue and he had actually to apologise through his Prime Minister to the plain men and women for trying to do his duty as a King to prevent a civil war! In fact, the actual rulers of Europe today have become mere expensive ornamental figures as the figures on a seal with which Government official documents are stamped. Thus being mere ornamental figures without any say or will of their own as far as the government of their countries is concerned, how can it be said, that the actual rulers of Europe are responsible for this war?

Let us next examine the soldiers whom Professor Dickinson and everybody now denounces for being responsible for this war. Ruskin in addressing the cadets at Woolwich, says: "The fatal error of modern institutions is to take away the best blood and strength of the nation, all the soul substance of it, that is brave, and careless of reward and scornful of pain and faithful in trust; and to cast that into steel and make a mere sword of it, *taking away its voice and will*; but to keep the worst part of the nation, whatever is cowardly, avaricious, sensual, and faithless, and to give to this the authority, to this the chief privilege where there is the least capacity of thought." "The fulfilment of your vow for the defence of England," Ruskin went on to say addressing the soldiers of Great Britain, "will by no means consist in carrying out such a system. You are no true soldiers if you only mean to *stand at a shop door to protect shop boys who are cheating in-side*." Now Englishmen, and true English soldiers too, who denounce Militarism and Prussian Militarism, I think, should read and ponder over these words of Ruskin. But what I want to say here is that it is evident from what Ruskin says here, that if the actual rulers in Europe have practically no say, the soldiers of Europe today have absolutely no say whatever in the government and conduct of affairs in their countries. What Tennyson says of the British soldiers at Bala-clava, is true of the poor soldiers now in this war, "Theirs was not to reason why, theirs was but to do and die." In fact if the acutal rulers in Europe today have become mere expensive ornamental figures, the soldiers in Europe now have become mere dangerous mechanical au-tomatons. Being more mechanical automatons without any voice or will of their own as far as the government of their countries is con-cerned, how then can it be said that the soldiers in Europe are respon-sible for this war?

Last of all, let us examine the case against the diplomats now in Europe. Now, according to the theories of Government, the Magua Chartas of Liberty and Constitutions of Europe, the diplomats—the actual Statesmen and Ministers in charge of the government and con-duct of public affairs in a country now are there merely to carry out the will of the people: in other words, merely to do whatever the plain men and women in the country tell them to do. Thus we see that the diplomats,—the Statesmen and Ministers in the Government of the countries in Europe today, have also become mere machines, talking machines; in fact mere puppets as in a Marionnettes show; puffed-up puppets without any will of their own, worked, pulled and moved up and down by the plain men and women. Being mere hollow puffed-up puppets, with only a voice, but without any will of their own, how then can it be said that the diplomats,—the Statesmen and Ministers now in European countries are responsible for this war?

Indeed the most curious thing, it seems to me, in the govern-ment of all the European countries today is that every one who is ac-tually in charge of the conduct of affairs in the Government,—ruler, soldier as well as diplomat or Statesman and Minister, is not allowed to have any will of his own; not allowed to have any power to do what he thinks best for the security and good of the nation, but every plain man and woman,—John Smith, editor of the "Patriotic Times,"

Bobus of Houndsditch, once in Carlyle's time, sausage maker and jam manufacturer, but now owner of a big Dreadnought ship building yard, and Moses Lump, money lender, —are given full power to have all their will and all the say in the government of the country; in fact, the power to tell the actual ruler, soldier and diplomat what they are to do for the good and security of the nation. Thus you will find, if you go deep enough into the matter, that it is these three persons, —John Smith, Bobus of Houndsditch and Moses Lump, who are responsible for this war. For it was these three persons, John Smith, Bobus and Moses Lump, I want to point out here, who created that monstrous modern Machine, —the modern Militarism in Europe, and it was this monstrous Machine which has brought on this war.

But now it will be asked why have the actual rulers, soldiers and diplomats of Europe so cowardly abdicated in favour of these three persons, John Smith, Bobus and Moses Lump? I answer, because the plain men and women, —even the good honest plain men and women, such men as Professor Dickinson, —instead of giving their loyalty and support to the actual rulers, soldiers and diplomats of their country, have taken the side of John Smith, Bobus and Moses Lump against their own rulers, soldiers and diplomats. The two reasons again why the plain men and women in Europe support and take the side of John Smith, Bobus and Moses Lump, are: first, because John Smith, Bobus and Moses Lump tell the plain men and women that they John Smith, Bobus and Moses Lump belong to the party of plain men and women; and, secondly, because the plain men and women in Europe from their childhood have been taught that the *Nature of Man is evil*; that every man, whenever he is invested with power, will abuse his power; and further that every man as soon as he gets strong enough to be able to do it, will be sure to want to rob and murder his neighbour. In fact, I want to say here the reason why John

Smith, Bobus and Moses Lump have been able to get the plain men and women in Europe to help them to force the actual rulers, soldiers and diplomats of Europe to create the monstrous modern machine, which has brought on this terrible war, is because the plain men and women in every country, when in a crowd, are always selfish and cowardly.

Thus, if you go into the root of the matter, you will see that it is not the rulers, soldiers and diplomats, not even John Smith, Bobus and Moses Lump, but it is really the good honest plain men and women, such men as Professor Dickison himself, who are responsible for this war. But Professor Dickinson will repudiate and say: We plain men and women did not want this war. But then, who wanted this war? I answer, Nobody wanted this war. Well then, what brought on this war? I answer, It was panic which brought on this war; the panic of the mob, — the panic which seized and took possession of the crowd of plain men and women in all European countries when last August that monstrous modern machine in Russia which the plain men and women had helped to create, began to move. In short, it was panic, I say, — the panic of the mob, panic of the crowd of the plain men and women communicating itself to and seizing and paralysing the brains of the rulers, soldiers and diplomats of the countries now at war and making them helpless which has brought on this terrible war. Thus we see, it was not, as Professor Dickinson says, the rulers, soldiers and diplomats, who have conducted and led the plain men and women of Europe into this catastrophe, but it was the plain men and women, — the selfishness, the cowardice and at the last moment, the funk, the panic of the plain men and women who have driven and pushed the poor helpless rulers, soldiers and diplomats of Europe into this catastrophe, —into this hell of a war. Indeed the tragic hopelessness of the situation now in Europe I want to say here, lies in the abject, pitiful, pitiable helplessness of the actual rulers, soldiers and diplomats of the countries now at war at the present moment.

It is evident therefore from what I have shown in the above, that if there is to be peace in Europe now and in the future, the first thing to be done is not, as Professor Dickinson says, to bring or call in, but to remove and keep out the plain men and women who, when in a crowd, are so selfish and cowardly; who are so liable to panic whenever the question of peace and war arises. In other words, if there is to be peace in Europe, the first thing to be done, it seems to me, is to protect the rulers, soldiers and diplomats from the plain men and women; to protect them from the mob, —the panic of the crowd of plain men and women which makes them helpless. In fact, not to speak of the future, if the present actual situation now in Europe is to be saved, the only way to do it, it seems to me, is first to rescue the rulers, soldiers and diplomats of the countries now at war, from their present helplessness. The tragic hopelessness of the situation now in Europe, I wish to point here, is that everybody wants peace, but nobody has the courage or power to make peace. I say therefore, the first thing to be done is to rescue the rulers, soldiers and diplomats from their present helplessness; to find some means to give them *power*, — power to find a way to make peace. That, I think, can be done only in one way and that is for the people of Europe, —for the people of the countries now at war, to tear up their present Constitutions and Magna Chartas of Liberty, and make a new Magna, Charta—a *Magna Charta of Loyalty*—such as we Chinese have in our Religion of good citizenship here in China.

By this new Magna Charta of Loyalty, the people of the countries now at war must swear: first not to discuss, meddle or interfere in any way with the politics of the present war; secondly, absolutely to accept, submit to and abide by whatever terms of peace their actual rulers may decide upon among themselves. This new Magna Charta of Loyalty, will at once give the actual rulers of the countries now at war *power* and, with power, courage to make peace; in fact, power and courage at once to order and command peace. I am perfectly sure that as soon as this power is given them, the actual rulers of the countries now at war, will at once order and command peace. I say, I am perfectly sure of this, because the rulers of the countries now at war, unless they are absolute incurable lunatics or demons, which everybody must admit that they are not, —no, not even, I will venture to say here, the most slandered man now in Europe, the Emperor of Germany, —they, the rulers of the countries now at war, must see that for them together to continue to spend nine million pounds sterling of the blood and sweat-earned money of their people everyday in order to slaughter the lives of thousands of innocent men and to destroy the homes and happiness of thousands of innocent women, is really nothing but *infernal madness*. The reason why the rulers, soldiers and diplomats of the countries now at war cannot see this, is because they feel themselves helpless; helpless before the panic of the mob, —the panic of the crowd of plain men and women; in fact, as I said because the panic of the crowd, —the panic of the mob has seized and paralysed their brains. I say therefore the first thing to be done, if the present actual situation now in Europe is to be saved, is to rescue the rulers, soldiers and diplomats of the countries now at war from the panic of the mob, —the panic of the crowd of plain men and women by giving them power.

The tragic hopelessness of the situation now in Europe, I want to say here further, lies not only in the helplessness of the rulers, soldiers and diplomats, but also in the helplessness of everybody in the countries now at war. Everybody is helpless and cannot see that this war, wanted by nobody and brought on only by the panic of the mob, is an infernal madness, because, as I said, the panic of the mob has seized and paralysed the brains of everybody. One can see this even in Professor Dickinson, who writes to inveigh against the war,

—to denounce the rulers, soldiers and diplomats for bringing on this war. Professor Dickinson too, without being conscious of it, has the panic of the mob in his brain. He begins his article by stating that this article of his is not a "stop the war" paper. He goes on to say: "Being in the war, I think, as all Englishmen think, we must go on fighting until we can emerge from it with our terroritory and security intact and with the future peace of Europe assured as far as human wisdom can assure it." The integrity and security of the British Empire and the future peace of Europe to be obtained only by going on indefinitely spending nine million pounds sterling of good money and slaughtering thousands of innocent men everyday! The monstrous absurdity of such a proposition, I believe, has only to be stated, to be seen by any one who has not the panic of the mob in his brain. The peace of Europe! Why, I think if this rate of spending and slaughtering goes on for any length of time, there will certainly be peace, but no Europe left on the map of the world. Indeed if there is anything which will show how really and utterly unfit the plain men and women are to decide on the question of peace and war, this attitude of mind of a man even like Professor Dickinson conclusively shows it.

But the point I want to insist upon here, is that everybody even in the countries now at war wants peace, but nobody has the *power* to make peace, to stop the war. Now the fact that nobody has the power to make peace, to stop the war, makes everybody believe that there is no possible way of making peace; makes everybody despair of the possibility of making peace. *This despair of the possibility of making peace* it is which prevents everybody in the countries now at war from seeing that this war wanted by nobody and brought on only by the panic of the mob, is really nothing but an infernal madness. The first thing to be done, therefore, in order to make everybody see that this war is nothing but an infernal madness is to show everybody that there *is a possibility of making peace*. In order to make everybody see that there is a possibility of making peace, the very first and simple thing to do is at once to stop the war; to invest some one with full power to stop the war; to invest the rulers of the countries now at war with *absolute power* by making, as I said, a Magna Charta of Loyalty, —absolute power to order and command the war to be stopped at once. As soon as everybody sees that the war *can* be stopped, everybody in the countries now at war, everybody except perhaps a few absolute incurable lunatics, will be able to see that this war wanted by nobody and brought on only by the panic of the mob, —is really nothing but an infernal madness; that this war, if continued, will be ruinous even to the countries which will emerge victorious from it. As soon as the rulers of the countries now at war have the power to stop the war and everybody in the countries now at war sees and realises that this war is an infernal madness, it will then and *only then* be not only possible, but easy for a man like President Wilson of the United States to make a successful appeal, as the Ex-President Roosevelt did during the Russo-Japanese war, to the rulers of the countries now at war to order and command the war to be stopped at once and then to find a way to make a permanent peace. I say it will be easy then for a man like President Wilson to make a *successful* appeal for peace because, I believe, in order to make peace, the only important thing the rulers of the countries now at war will have to do is, to build a special lunatic asylum and arrest and clap into it the few absolute incurable lunatics, —men like Professor Dickinson who have the panic of the mob in the brain, —the panic for the integrity and security of the British Empire and the future peace of Europe!

Thus, I say, the one and only way out of this war, is for the people of the countries now at war, to tear up their present Magna Chartas of Liberty and Constitutions, and make a new Magna Charta, a Magna Charta not of Liberty, but a Magna Charta of Loyalty, such as we Chinese have in our Religion of good citizenship here in China.

To prove the efficacy of what I now propose, let me here call the attention of the people of Europe and America to the fact that it was the *absolute loyalty* of the people of Japan and Russia to their rulers which made it possible for the Ex-President Roosevelt to make a successful appeal to the late Emperor of Japan and the present Emperor of Russia to stop the Russo-Japanese war and to command and order the peace to be made at Portsmouth. This absolute loyalty of the people in the case of Japan is secured by the Magna Charta of Loyalty in our Chinese Religion of good citizenship which the Japanese learnt from us. But in Russia where there is no Religion of good citizenship with its Magna Charta of Loyalty, the absolute loyalty of the Russian people has to be secured by the power of the *Knout*.

Now see what happened, after the Treaty of Portsmouth, in a country with a Religion of good citizenship and its Magna Charta of Loyalty, like Japan, and a country without such a Religion and such a Charta like Russia. In Japan, after the Treaty of Portsmouth, the plain men and women in Tokyo whose Religion of good citizenship had been spoilt by the New Learning of Europe, raised a clamour and tried to create a panic, —but the Magna Charta of Loyalty in the hearts of the true unspoilt Japanese people with the help of a few policemen in one day put down the clamour and panic of the plain men and women and there has been not only internal peace in Japan but peace in the Far East ever since. * But in Russia after the Treaty of Portsmouth, the plain men and women everywhere in the country, also raised a clamour and tried to create a panic, and, because there is no Religion of good citizenship in Russia, the *Knout*, —which secured the abso-

---

* Peace in the Far East, I say, until lately the mob-worshipping Statesmen of Great Britain got their apt pupils the now also mob-worshipping Statemen of Japan, men like Count Okuma, who is the greatest mob-worshipper now in Japan, —to make war against a handful of German clerks in Tsingtau!

lute loyalty of the Russian people, *broke* and thus ever since the plain men and women in Russia have had full liberty to make riots and Constitutions, to raise clamour and create panic. — panic for the integrity and security of the Russian Empire and the Slavonic race and for the future peace of Europe! The result of all this was that when a petty difference of opinion arose between the Austrian Emperor and the Emperor of Russia over the degree of punishment to be meted out for the people responsible for the murder of the Austrian Arch-Duke, the plain men and women, the mob in Russia were able to raise such a clamour and create such a panic for the integrity and security of the Russian Empire, that the Emperor of Russia and his immediate advisers were driven to mobilise the whole Russian army, in other words, to move that monstrous modern machine created by John Smith, Bobus and Moses Lump. When that monstrous modern machine, — the modern Miliarism in Russia, began to move, there was immediately a general panic among the plain men and women in all Europe and it was this general panic among the plain men and women in Europe seizing and paralysing the brains of the rulers and diplomats of the countries now at war and making them helpless, which, as I have already shown, brought on this terrible war.

Thus the real origin of this war, if you go deep into the very root of the matter, was the Treaty of Portsmouth. I say the Treaty of Portsmouth was origin of this war, because after that Treaty, the *Knout*, — the power of the Knout, — in Russia *broke* and there was nothing to protect the Emperor of Russia from the plain men and women, — from the panic of the crowd of plain men and women, — in fact, from the panic of the mob in Russia, — the panic of the mob for the integrity and security of the Russian Empire and the Slavonic race! The German poet Heine with wonderful insight considering that he was the most liberal of all Liberals, in fact the Champion of the Liberalism of his time, says: "The Absolutism in Russia is really a

Dictatorship rather than anything else with which to bring into life and make possible the carrying out of the liberal ideas of our modern times (der Absolutismus in Russland ist vielmehr eine Dictatur um die liberalen Ideen unserer neuesten Zeit in's Leben treten zu lassen)". In fact, I say again, after the Treaty of Portsmouth the Dictatorship, —the *Knout*, the power of the Knout in Russia *broke* and there was nothing to protect the ruler, soldier and diplomat of Russia from the mob, —that, I say, was the real origin of this war. In other words, the real origin and cause of this war was the *fear of the mob in Russia*.

In Europe in the past the responsible rulers of all the European countries were able to maintain civil order in their own countries and to keep international peace in Europe, because they feared and worshipped God. But now, I want to say, the rulers, soldiers and diplomats in all European countries of today instead of fearing and worshipping God, fear and worship the mob, —fear and worship the crowd of plain men and women in their country. The Russian Emperor, Alexander I, who made the Holy Alliance in Europe after the Napoleonic wars, was able not only to maintain civil order in Russia, but to keep international peace in Europe because he feared God. But the present Emperor in Russia is not able to maintain civil order in his own country and to keep international peace in Europe, because, instead of fearing God, he fears the mob. In Great Britain rulers like Cromwell, were able to maintain civil order in their own country and to keep international peace in Europe, because they worshipped God. But the actual rulers of Great Britain today, responsible Statesmen like Lord Grey, Messrs. Asquith, Churchill and Loyd George, are not able to maintain civil order in their own country and keep international peace in Europe, because, instead of worshipping God, they worship the mob, —worship not only the mob in their own country, but also the mob in other countries. The late Prime Minister of Great Britain

Mr. Campbell Bannerman, when the Russian Duma was dissolved, shouted at the top of his voice, "*Le Duma est mort. Vive le Duma!*"

I have said that the real origin and cause of this war was the fear of the mob in Russia. Now I want to say here that, the real *first* origin and cause of this war was not the fear of the mob in Russia. The first origin and cause, —the *fons et origo* not only of this war, but of all the anarchy, horror and misery in the world today, —is the worship of the mob, the worship of the mob now in all European countries and in America, —especially in Great Britain. It was the worship of the mob in Great Britain which caused and brought on the Russo-Japanese war. * After the Russo-Japanese war came the Treaty of Portsmouth and the Treaty of Portsmouth, with the help of the shout of the British Prime Minister, broke the *Knout*, —the power of the Knout, broke what Heine calls the Dictatorship and created the fear of the mob in Russia which, as I said, has brought on this terrible war. It is, I may incidentally say here, this worship of the mob in Great Britain, this worship of the mob among Englishmen and foreigners in China; in fact this Religion of the worship of the mob imported from Great Britain and America into China, —which has brought on the Revolution and the present nightmare of a Republic in China now threatening to destroy the most valuable asset of civilisation of the world today, the real Chinaman. I say therefore that this worship of the mob in Great Britain—this Religion of the worship of the mob in Europe and America today, unless it is at once put down, will destroy not only the civilisation of Europe, but all civilisation in the world.

---

* The panic of the mob in Great Britain, —especially the selfish panic of the British mob in Shanghai and in China whose mouthpiece then was the "great" Dr. Morrison, the "Times" correspondent in Peking, with their shout for the "open door" in Manchuria alarmed and incited the Japanese into the Russo-Japanese war.

Now, I say, the only thing, it seems to me, which can and will put down this worship of the mob, this Religion of the worship of the mob which now threatens to destroy all civilisation in the world today—is this Religion of Loyalty,—the Sacrament, the Magna Charta of Loyalty such as we Chinese have in our Religion of good citizenship here in China. This Magna Charta of Loyalty will protect the responsible rulers, soldiers and diplomats of all countries from the mob, and enable them not only to maintain civil order in their own countries but also to keep peace in the world. What is more, this Magna Charta of Loyalty,—this Religion of good citizenship with its Magna Charta of Loyalty, by enabling all good men and true to help their legitimate rulers to awe and keep down the mob—will enable the rulers of all countries to keep peace and maintain order in their own countries and in the world without the Knout, without policeman, without soldier; in one word without militarism.

Now before I conclude, I want to say a word about militarism, about German militarism. I have said that the first origin and cause of this war was the worship of the mob in Great Britain. Now I want to say here that if the first origin and cause of this war was the worship of the mob in Great Britain, the *direct* and immediate cause of this war was the *worship of might* in Germany. The Emperor of Russia is reported to have said before he signed the order for the mobilisation of the Russian army, "We have stood this for seven years. Now it must finish." These passionate words of the Emperor of Russia show how much he and the Russian nation must have suffered from the worship of might of the German nation. Indeed the worship of the mob in Great Britain, as I said, broke the *Knout* in the hands of the Emperor of Russia which made him helpless against the mob who wanted war and the worship of might of the German nation made him lose his temper which drove him to go in with the mob for war. Thus we see the real cause of this war was the worship of the mob in Great Britain and the worship of might in Germany. The Bible in our Chinese Religion of good citizenship says : "*Do not go against what is right, to get the praise of the people. Do not trample upon the wishes of the people to follow your own desires.* " * Now to go against what is right to get the praise of the people, is what I have called the worship of the mob, and to trample upon the wishes of the people to follow your own desires, is what I have called the worship of might. But with this Magna Charta of Loyalty, the responsible ministers and Statesmen in a country will feel themselves responsible not to the mob, not to the crowd of plain men and women, but *to their King and their Conscience*, and this will protect them from the temptation to go against what is right to get the praise of the people, —in fact protect them from mob worship. The Magna Charta of Loyalty again will make the rulers of a country feel the awful responsibility which the great power given them by Magna Charta of Loyalty imposes upon them and this will protect them from the temptation to trample upon the wishes of the people to follow their own desires, —in fact protect them from the worship of might. Thus we see this Magna Charta of Loyalty, —this Religion of good citizenship with its Magna Charta of Loyalty, will help to put down the worship of the mob and the worship of might, which, as I have shown, are the cause of this war.

The French Joubert who had lived through the French Revolution in answer to the modern cry for liberty said: "Let your cry be for free souls rather than for free men. Moral liberty is the one vitally important liberty, the liberty which is indispensible; the other liberty is good and salutary only so far as it favours this. *Subordination is in*

---

* 罔违道以干百姓之誉
  罔拂百姓以从己之欲
(Shu-king or Canon of History in the Confucian Bible: Part II ch. 1.6.)

itself a better thing than independance. The one implies order and arrangement; the other implies only self sufficiency with isolation. The one means harmony, the other, a single tone; the one, is the whole, the other is but the part."

This then, I say, is the one and only way for the people of Europe, for the people of the countries now at war, not only to get out of this war, but to save the civilisation of Europe, —to save the civilisation of the world, and that is for them now to tear up their present Magna Chartas of liberty and Constitutions, and make a new Magna Charta, —a Magna Charta not of liberty, but a Magna Charta of Loyalty; in fact to adopt the Religion of good citizenship with its Magna Charta of Loyalty such as we Chinese have here in China.

AB INTEGRO SAECLORUM NASCITUR ORDO! *

---

* 世纪的秩序将重新诞生